THE BIG CON

THE BIG CON

How I stole £30 million and got away with it

Tony Sales

MIRROR BOOKS

First published by Mirror Books in 2020
Mirror Books is part of Reach plc
10 Lower Thames Street
London EC3R 6EN
England

www.mirrorbooks.co.uk

ISBN 978-1913406394

Printed and bound in Great Britain by
CPI Group (UK) Ltd, Croydon, CR0 4YY

A CIP catalogue record for this book is available from the British Library.

NOTE:

Some names and details have been changed to protect the guilty.

For Nan and Grandad

Contents

	Introduction	1
	Prologue: Notes from a Bank Heist	3
1	Greenwich	8
2	Little Tramp	17
3	My First Scam	26
4	Robbing Lenny McLean	34
5	Computers Don't Commit Crime – People Do	41
6	Revenge	51
7	Monty	54
8	Building a Team	59
9	The Job Interview	64
10	Sweet Seventeen	68
11	Moving Out of Greenwich	73
12	Crime Tips from the Old Bill	79
13	Star Seller	84
14	Greenwich Again	88
15	Phone Shop	90
16	Buy Now, Pay Never	100
17	The Counterfeiters	110

18 Meet the Team   116
19 Cocaine & the Night Club Incident   127
20 Belmarsh Prison   133
21 Freedom   142
22 Bristol   146
23 The Yacht   153
24 Here's Johnny   157
25 Meet the Yardies   164
26 The Great Car Robberies   170
27 Mortgage Fraud: A Mexican Stand Off   179
28 Nicked Again   187
29 Interrogation   190
30 Keyser Soze   203
31 On the Run   213
32 Teething Problems   217
33 The Cult of Power   229
34 Radio & the Beginning of the End   234
35 Visiting Permission   237
36 The Road to Going Straight   253
37 Home Office   256
38 A New Man   260
39 Retail Risk   266
40 Nan   270
41 The Passport   274
42 The Boxer & Nearly Losing Everything   279
43 No Knock this Time   283
44 Underworld TV   291
45 Andy   295
46 Solomon   297
47 Endgame   303

THE BIG CON

Introduction

As the head of a crime syndicate and working alone, I robbed everyone, from banks to jewellers. I cleared out entire shopping centres and high streets with my team. And I ripped off plenty of other criminals too.

Even though I set out to avoid violent crime, I've fired guns and had them fired at me. I've ripped off shady accountants with Nigerian gangsters and kidnapped lawyers with some of the scariest motherfuckers on the planet.

To survive, I've assumed hundreds, if not thousands of identities. I fled more homes than most landlords will ever own. Learning to cheat from a young age, I became so adept at deception that even my own family didn't know I was living as a fugitive for half a decade.

Across my criminal career, which started at the age of seven and ended in my thirties, I stole well over £30 million. The media has labelled me Britain's Greatest Fraudster.

But I'm not telling this story to boast (I'm not proud of the things I did) or to cash in on the public's interest in crime (the profits from this book will go toward helping young people out of crime). Mine is a story that has many lessons – from how people are conned to how we, as a society, understand criminals and crime.

I might not have realised it at the time, because I thought I was just being clever – but the criminal mind nearly always develops from trauma. You could say I spent my whole life on the run, trying to escape, and I thought crime was the key to my freedom. But the truth is, even if they manage to evade the law, as I have done on plenty of occasions, criminals rarely get away. Happy endings are far and few between. So I'm writing this as a case study. You might not like me after you've read it – I've not edited out things that make me look bad. But I would ask you to read it with an open mind to the idea that if we give people the right support at a very early age, they won't go down the road I went down, and if they do, they can still change.

PROLOGUE

Notes from a Bank Heist

It's nine o'clock on a freezing London morning, and I'm staking out a bank. It's on the ground floor of a 10-floor office block around the corner from one of the busiest Overground stations in the outer zones. I press play and the music starts. I feel it wash over me; the rhythm kicks in and I start to relax. Dr Dre always does this to me. In my trance-like state, the building in front of me comes into focus. It is walled off, with a guard post for vehicles to go in and out. There is CCTV mounted at all the vantages, on corners and above doors. I am sitting there with my long scraggly beard and woolly hat, with a homeless guy's dog, just watching, unnoticed… In return for borrowing his spot and his dog, I've left him eating a nice breakfast with all the trimmings – sausage, egg, bacon, coffee and orange juice. I've also booked him a room for a week at a top-notch hotel. He has let me use his dog and his spot for a few hours this week, no questions asked, and I am grateful for that.

As staff are arriving for work, swiping their access cards sleepy-eyed, I am watching. An upstairs window is open, and will likely stay open, just like it did last night. But I know already that I won't be going in that way.

"Hullo," I say to the unsuspecting letting agent on the phone in a broad northern accent. "I'm at 18 [Redacted] Road. Would it be possible to view the space to rent on the 10th floor today? If it's not too much trouble, aye."

After a quick trip to the barbers, I go and meet Solomon in McDonald's. He's in his Hi-Viz jacket, polishing off his breakfast after a long night staking out one of the bank's employees. "It's confirmed," I tell him, relieved. "We're going in a couple of hours to view the property. Let's prepare ourselves."

Andy, our team leader, is waiting at the hotel room with a change of clobber for me and Sol: two very nice Savile Row suits, made to measure. Andy hands me and Solomon our business cards and mobile phones. We all have lanyards with our pictures and false names on them. We have even branded them with logos in the company name that we have made up. We all hop in the black Range Rover, looking like something out of *Men in Black*.

As we arrive, the guard leaves his post to usher us in through the gate. "Three minutes Solomon stalled him for," Andy notes. Human vulnerability is something that exists everywhere: the gate post guard likes to talk a bit. Sol has found out his favourite football team by doing some intelligence gathering, and now Sol is coincidentally also QPR's biggest fan. The guard is completely unaware that we are socially engineering him to behave the way we want him to.

While Sol talks to him on the driver's side, I slip out of the back passenger door and into the guard's office. I open the drawer and clone the access-all-areas card using a wireless grabber. The card has been left just sitting in his top drawer – something I had spotted a week earlier when setting off the fire alarms. I walk out to the front of the building; the guard doesn't spot me. It has worked like a dream, just like we planned it.

Sol and Andy park the car and we meet the letting agent by the gate post. He ushers us into the reception area. The space we're looking at is on the 10th floor, and on the way up there, we deliberately lose Solomon. There is CCTV all over the place, but Sol will be able to hack into those later and remove any trace of us ever being here.

"This looks absolutely fine to me," I say to the agent, nosing around the empty floor. "I'll have to check with my CEO, but the location's perfect for our London base. Take my business card, but I'll probably be calling you later to confirm that we will be taking it."

The agent shows me out. He has not even realised that Sol is holed up in the staff loos and not with us anymore. That letting agent was just a tool for us to get Solomon in; they will never hear from me again.

Later that day, when the staff have all left work, Solomon comes out of hiding in the toilet cubicle. He's spent the day in there on his laptop, hacking into the Wi-Fi and cracking alarm codes. Andy and I approach the building, and I open the door with the cloned access-all-areas card from the guard's office. We take an after-hours tour of the bank's headquarters. Down the corridor, turning left, we soon have access to all the servers.

Back in the open-plan area, where the clerks and the compliance branch work, we scan the scene for traces of human error. It's everywhere. Pinned to the wall by the secretary's desk, next to a hand-drawn chart of workmates' birthdays, is a list of usernames and passwords. I snap a photo. On a coat hook, there's a staff access card on a lanyard. I copy it with the wireless grabber. These new ones are similar to the one I had when I was 15, but this one clones RFID access cards.

I rummage through the drawers in the finance director's office. Solomon comes in with a cup of tea, but I've got something a lot sweeter. A card I found in the credit controller's desk probably has access to the bank's own account. It even comes with the pin number written on a post-it note.

An hour or so later, we leave through the back door. We haven't taken any cash. We don't need to. That's not why we're here. Data is the new cash, and we just stole all of theirs!

Tomorrow morning, Andy, Sol and I will meet the CEO of that bank. He is going to find out who we are, and what we are all about. You see, this is what they have paid for: they want to understand exactly how their business looks through the eyes of criminals. My previous life is not something I am at all proud of, but all the experience I gained gives me an extremely valuable commodity today. In the wrong hands, my skills can only satisfy greed and selfish desires. But while in prison in

2010, I saw my past in a totally new light. So I turned my life around by using my skills and experience to prevent the crimes I had once perpetrated.

People in my new profession often say to me, "I try to think like a criminal." They think that's the way to catch one. But my reaction is always the same: "Sorry to hear that." I say I'm sorry to hear that because the mind of a criminal is not always a happy place to be. It's a lonely, anxious, scary world, full of trauma. You can't just think like a criminal; it can't be taught. There are plenty of degrees in criminology, but there are no university courses in *criminality*.

There are an infinite number of ways the environment in which someone lives, the things which happen to them and their individual biology come together to create a criminal mind: that special combination of ruthlessness, outsider mentality and anger which causes so much chaos in the world. But there are common threads and many lessons we are learning to prevent that happening. What you are about to read is the story of how *I* developed a criminal mind. How I rose through the ranks of south London's criminal underworld, from being used in robberies aged seven, to running my own crime empire, with hundreds of people working for me. And how I have turned that mind to good, to help prevent crime today.

CHAPTER ONE

Greenwich

I was born on 11 January 1974 in Greenwich District Hospital, south-east London, to my mum Kim and dad Louis. When I was two days old, my mum, aged just 17, under pressure to work, gave me to my nan to be looked after. A year later my dad would leave my mum, and I would become just another statistic of abandonment. Researchers have discovered that when a parent leaves during the first five years of a child's life, they are 52 percent more likely to go on to have an addiction in adulthood. Not one to disappoint, I developed my first addiction aged just seven: crime. I don't think that anyone could have looked at me as a small baby, passed between my mum and nan, and have predicted what I would become even before the age of 10.

One of my first memories is sitting in the back yard at my nan's, when I was passed over the fence to her neighbour Nel. My mum was trying to take me away from my nan, who wouldn't give me up, or let her come back to the house. She was very strong like that, my nan:

"You've made your bed; you must lie in it."

Sometimes my mum would make me live with her in a squat somewhere with whoever she appeared to have hooked up with at the time. When I was two years old, she got so drunk one night that she let me grab the electric bar on the fire and hold it, screaming, until she woke up. On another occasion, I poured a boiling pan of water onto myself because she wasn't watching me. Mum would always take me back from my nan, because she wanted to start a new family life. But then my nan would come around and save me from her, and the cycle of "pass Tony around" would start all over again.

My dad dipped in and out of my life, but he was getting on with his own new life and didn't need a kid around his neck like a dead weight. Being passed back and forth like moody goods, coupled with screaming and fights, was enough to give anybody endless hang-ups.

Nan owned Shirley's Hair Fashions, a hairdressers' at 153 Trafalgar Road, Greenwich. I grew up in that shop, and it holds beautiful memories for me. Nan was always messing about with my hair. She would dye it and perm it, put highlights in, put rubber caps on my head, pull my hair through and bleach it, leaving the parts that she pulled through bright blonde.

I didn't go to a proper barber's until I was 11 or 12. My mates were all getting their hair shaved, and it was something I wanted, but my nan was a women's hairdresser and didn't know how to use clippers. She was more into doing blue rinses and perms.

My uncle Shaun Kelly, my mum's brother who was 10 years older, lived at the house, and he was the first male that I bonded with growing up. My grandad worked as a plumber, but I much preferred hanging out with my nan at her salon, sitting around with the old ladies and smoking fags. They used to put the fags in my mouth and light them.

My mum also worked as a hairdresser, but in a different salon. She got a flat on Cherry Orchard Estate, which is now quite notorious, in Charlton. Back then my mum was a drinker. She was young when she had me, so she preferred to be out partying while my nan looked after me. They would always argue over me. My mum would use me as an emotional weapon against my nan. She would come and take me away, saying I was *her* kid, even though she was still a kid herself. They would have massive arguments about my mum taking me out too late, or going around somebody's house to get drunk.

When I was eight or nine, my nan got full custody of me. My mum and dad signed it over. This was mostly because my mum had decided to marry a man called John Nelson. My nan didn't want him around me: she called him Beater Basher, because she knew he was violent to women. One of the women who got her hair done in Nan's shop had previously been married to him.

My mum married him around 1984 while I was at primary school. It only lasted 18 months, but it was disruptive and horrific. My school, Meridian, made me have hearing tests because they thought I couldn't hear and was deaf. In reality, I just wasn't paying attention in class because of what was going on at home. But I didn't want to tell them about it. What could I have said? "My mum's new husband is beating the shit out of her, and there's nothing I can do." I could imagine their reaction: they would take me away again, not back to my nan's, but somewhere else, with strangers. Perhaps I'd be put in care. The thought scared me.

My nan cooked homemade dinners every day, so there was always meat and vegetables, always food on the table. I only ate at dinner time, I never got snacks or treats. Our house always smelt of home cooking. There was no junk food at my nan's place: she didn't believe in convenience food. The furthest she went was ready salted crisps, or on a Monday she'd buy two sausage rolls from Kennedys. At a push, I could have one of them with a bit of salad cream. I never had McDonald's because we weren't allowed to eat it, but we could have what she called a "Black Chef" – a KFC. I don't know why she called it that, but I suspected it was because they had Indian people working as chefs. That was the only time I ever heard her refer to race in any shape or form. Most of my mates were black guys who I had more in common with than the other white kids that I knew. Racism was everywhere; they had been through so much abuse, and I guess that was relatable to me.

I was knocking about with a kid called Stephen Pye, whose mum and dad were friends of my mum. When I was staying with my mum, and my nan was away somewhere, they would come back to have a drink at the house. And it was on one of those days that Stephen turned to me with a steely look in his eye. "I'm going to the shop, because I'm hungry and you've not got any food that I eat."

I went with him, and he nicked some fish paste. It was the first time I'd seen anyone steal anything, and it taught me that you could nick things you don't have in your house.

Where I came from, in south London – the dirty south – it was quite trendy to be naughty. Breaking the rules and being bad was something people found inherently interesting, especially if they didn't dare to do it themselves. That's why south London was called "bandit country": everyone was a bandit! From the outside, there was glamour to villains, and I grew up around them. They were the local legends and lore. Most crime is committed by working-class people. Poverty and trauma are the main drivers of crime, globally: both are everywhere in the working-class world. I was a little fucker born into a working-class family, banking childhood trauma right up until I was 15.

Do you know how many women used to complain about my behaviour to my nan in the salon? "I saw him nicking, I saw him smoking, I saw him smashing a car window." One even said she saw me sniffing glue. My nan told me endless stories about things I'd done – even if I hadn't done them! I was constantly told, "You stole this, you did that, where's your moral code?" They had already decided who I was. Give a man a role to play and he'll play it. So, I did.

It wasn't as if I was surrounded by bad people all the

time. My grandad was the sweetest man in the world. He was unassuming and wouldn't hurt a fly, although he was frequently surrounded by mischief. The house was full of my nan's spectacular furniture that we weren't allowed to sit on. She had a big French dresser full of crystal ornaments and lots of frilly lace everywhere, and I can still remember the smell of hairspray on her blonde beehive hair. When I was very young, we had a psychotic poodle called Suzie who got nicked out of our front yard. We also had a big green Amazonian parrot called Big Bird. Big Bird hated men but loved women, especially my nan. Living in Greenwich around so many criminals, Big Bird must have learned to imitate them. He knew how to escape from his cage, and he was pretty violent too. He would fling the brass plaques my nan had hung everywhere around the house at my grandad. In hindsight, mine might be a rare case of a boy imitating a parrot, because I went on to copy most of his naughty behaviour.

We used to have to hide from debt collectors. My nan had paid £1,500 to buy her house, which is amazing when you consider that the same Victorian cottage is now worth over half a million. But she didn't have the money to pay it one week. It was Friday night and the man wanted his money. He was banging on the door, peering through the window while we all hid behind the sofa with the lights off.

Even though he was a good, honest, hardworking man, when times were tough my grandad drilled a hole through the electric meter to rig it. He figured out that when the engineers came round with a meter to test it, they'd hold a torch to the side of the meter. If the light went through, it shone on the disc that was spinning, and they knew you were cheating. So, we put a bit of chewing gum on the side of it to cover the gap and stop the light. It was a popular scam at the time – and it was the only way we could get by.

In the middle of Tyler Street, there was a swing park with a roundabout, and at the top there was a pub. At that time it was closed and under development. Pubs back then used to have off-licences attached to them, a little kiosk at the side, so people would go to the pub and get their booze to take away. The pub was on a street with a dead-end, next to a railway arch. It was called the Vanbrugh Tavern.

My uncle, who was only in his teens, was always hanging out there with the older boys, and my nan used to shoo me away from home, telling me, "Go and play with the big boys." One time, while I was playing with my mates around the railway line, exploring, building dens and eating the blackberries that grew along most of south London's train line tracks, my uncle called over to me: "Oi, come here." They said they wanted to lower me into the pub, which had a flat roof. They needed me because I was only 7 years old, so small but strong enough to do what they needed – they were all too big to fit through the gap. All I had to do was run to the front and open the door so they could get in. I already knew the layout, because I'd been into the kiosk and bought Mars bars and bottles of coke many times. They tied a rope around me like that scene in *Mission: Impossible* and lowered me through a hatch in the roof. Once I was in, I undid the rope, took it off, and opened the door to let them in.

Everyone had fags after that. As a reward for my part in the heist, the older boys gave me a pack. This was different from the old dears in my nan's hairdressers: I was smoking properly, lighting it myself. I had just committed a pretty serious crime for the first time, and got paid for it. It felt good. I felt acceptance from my peer group, and I liked it.

There's something that happens when you commit a crime with others. You create a special bond. In my world, that's trust. Then you do another job together, and you get to really trust them. For the first time, I was starting to build bonds that I didn't even have at home.

After I got lowered in, my uncle had said, "Don't say anything to Nan!"

But I was a kid who questioned things, so I asked him why.

"Because it's naughty, dickhead. Don't say anything. Shh!"

The criminal code of *omertà* was being drilled into me from a young age.

Whenever anyone gets caught in the criminal world, if you've been grafting with them, they will tell you, "I didn't say anything!" When somebody does grass, an iron fist comes down on them. The fear of this kind of punishment reverberates outside the circle.

When you are doing something illegal, you know that if you're not careful you can get locked up for it.

When I was younger, I was worried about getting locked up. I didn't want the police to know me, and I wanted to fit into society and be normal. That was all I ever wanted – to be normal. But growing up in chaos, I never stood a chance.

CHAPTER TWO

Little Tramp

As a kid, I always had massive amounts of energy. I could climb the PE frame the fastest. All the time I spent climbing walls and roofs down at the scrapyards, or jumping off cranes at the wimpy asphalt by the river, gave me a bit of an edge. I suspect I had ADHD or something of the sort, but back then people weren't aware of such conditions. If something was going on, I was in the thick of it. If I had been living in different circumstances – if agriculture had not taken our right to hunt away – I would have been Neanderthal ripped. My brain is wired for survival of the fittest, and I was the fittest.

I took risks that most people couldn't, and even back then I knew I was different from the other kids. Being surrounded by violence, mostly induced by alcohol, you learn how to cope in very stressful situations; it gives you lightning-quick reactions. Say the wrong thing in my world and it could lead to death. Words start wars. I learnt later that most criminals have a low resting heart rate: nature and nurture working perfectly together, just

17

like our ancestors who were hunters, stalking their prey.

While ADHD had me running all over the place, thinking differently didn't serve me as well in the classroom. One day at Meridian we were told to design a badge; the best design would become the school badge, and it would be put on all the uniforms. I remember looking at it at the time and thinking, *I haven't got a clue where to start!* That was the first time I had ever not known what to do next. I'd never really thought about structure or representation until that point.

They wanted us to represent that we were the school of Greenwich, the one with the Meridian line running right through it. But my mind was blank. I had stuff going on at home that was taking up most of the space in my brain. I sat there and stared at the paper, then at the wall, then out the window. I was mentally blocked. I didn't know how to structure it, and I was overthinking and ramping up the complexity of it. My mum was about to marry a monster – I'd heard all the adults around me saying he would kill her. But the teacher, Mr Hodges, thought I was simply too thick to understand it. He just wrote me off, grabbing me by the ears. "You're an idiot, Sales." He didn't even think to ask me why my page was blank.

After Mr Hodges grabbed me, the school sent me to a child psychologist. I had to go to a nice little park called The Pleasance every Thursday at 5.30 pm for interviews with a guy who would ask me questions. I'd always been taught not to talk to strangers. And I was an extremist in that regard. He was a stranger, so I wasn't going to tell him anything. Not one of them ever asked me, "Is there something going on at home? Is everything okay? Do you have any issues?" Not that they would have got anything out of me, because I'd shut down. I was non-responsive.

Regardless of my silence, the psychiatrists must have spotted that something was going on in my home life – perhaps my mum and dad splitting up was causing the problems at school – but they didn't really know what it was, so they couldn't act on it. I went there for a year, before they let me go, saying nothing was wrong with me. When I was 10, my nan battled and got me moved to Halstow School.

It didn't help that my mum was still set on getting married to Beater Basher. He was a lot older than her – 30-odd years older – had a few quid, and smoked a pipe. He had glasses and grey hair and was an evil-looking man. He lived at the back of my new school.

The first weekend that I went to stay with them, he gave me a tin box full of lighters. None of them had any gas in them, but they all had flints.

My mum had put her child within reach of a nutcase, a woman-beating psycho. But she didn't know any better, so I sat there playing with the lighters, flicking them, and the next thing I heard was slap! Bang! Crash! I was downstairs and I heard my mum shout, "No!" The next moment, he was beating the shit out of her. I mean, absolutely beating the shit out of her. Her head was swollen like a watermelon, and it wouldn't be the last time he'd do that.

Every time I went and stayed with my mum, I ended up listening to domestic violence. He already had kids from his ex-wife who he'd also beaten up. He didn't see them, and didn't want another one like me around. So he and mum would argue, and then that would lead to a fight, which in turn led to my mum getting smashed up again, all while I was in the house. Any man who thinks they can abuse a woman, especially while kids are there, is disgusting. A piece of shit. And he really was a piece of shit.

I liked my new school, Halstow, though. At Meridian, I had been teased because I had £1.99 plimsolls. Most of the other kids had the latest brands: Reebok, Adidas and of course Nike. My nan didn't know what Nikes were. She wasn't into all that. My grandparents had lived through the war, and so things like brands just seemed immaterial. But things were different at Halstow. There were other kids in the same boat as me. There was Sherry Phelan, who was my first girlfriend, the first person to ask me out, during a school trip to the Isle of Wight when I was 10. She had one sister, Kelly, and two brothers, Thomas and Nicki. That was the first time a girl ever took any interest in me. I would crave that for ages, because it didn't happen for a while after that. Looking at a picture of myself back then, I can see why.

At Halstow I also met two guys called Tony T and Paul C, who became some of my best mates. Paul was Scottish; his parents were globe trotters and had just moved from Canada to Greenwich. Marvin Booth was another guy I became good friends with. I started hanging around with these three more than anyone else. Danny Rogers and Danny Staples would come in and out of our crew. Paul and I were white, Marvin and Tony were black.

A boy called Stephen Parr, who was older, lived at the top of my road. He used to bully me because of who I was friends with, calling me a little tramp. "You smell, we don't want you around here. I hate you, fuck off." He probably had his own issues, because I never saw him with a dad. Maybe I was more relatable to him than he realised.

There were some other kids around the back side of Tyler Street who I was starting to hang around with: Martin Bingham, Stacey Melvin and his brother Mark, and Danny, Ben and Jamie Mitchell, who was one of the best-looking boys around. All the girls fancied him. He was brilliant at football and was the kid every boy wanted to be, including me. Jamie and his sister Lucy lived with their mum – he had no dad around, just like me. There was a girl called Zoe Rust who was stunning, and every boy fell in love with her. Her Dad used to do adverts, so we used to think she was famous.

Behind my nan's hairdressing shop was where they filmed the Krays films. Walking around there, you'd reach the river, and back then there were scrapyards. That was where we all used to hang about and get into all kinds of trouble together.

Although we didn't have lots of money, my nan used to save to go on holidays, so throughout my childhood, we did lots of travelling around the UK in a caravan, and on campsites. We created a racket and a ruckus wherever we went, one of those rowdy families that like to have fun. When we went to Clacton and stayed in a caravan, Nan took Big Bird away with us and he pecked through the air bed. She was asleep, snoring on it as it went down, and when she woke up it was flat as a pancake. There were fits of laughter. In Dorset, she got us thrown off the site over a fruit machine. Later we went to Cheddar with my new stepdad, a lovely honest fellow my mum had met while working in the pub as a barmaid. His name was John – another John – but he was a good bloke, who's still with my mum to this day.

Not long after my mum got together with good John, she fell pregnant. Nine months later I had a little sister, Kate. My nan dressed her in frilly lace and a bonnet, and bought a huge red pram to push her up and down Trafalgar Road in, like she was a porcelain doll.

Mum and Nan still argued, and stopped speaking for long periods at a time. Kate would come to stay with Nan, but when she had to go back she would cry her eyes out, "screaming blue murder", as Nan would say. I think my nan thought my mum was doing it on purpose, using Kate as an emotional weapon, like what had happened to me. I think my mum just wanted her own mum back. But Nan, being Nan, put her barriers up.

In Cheddar, I took John out in a boat, knowing he couldn't swim. I pushed him further and further out, kicking my legs. It was so deep; I'd swum so far out that I couldn't dive to the bottom. But I made sure he got back to shore okay. Because that's what I have always done: I might test the waters, see how far I can push the limits, but I always make sure the people I care about are safe.

Although my family were often pissed as farts, on the surface they were happy. I remember my mum bowling around with a peacock feather in the rain. "Oi mate," she said to a bloke trying to shelter under a newspaper, "do you wanna borrow my umbrella?" They were always up for a laugh, but when alcohol was involved the situation could explode at any time, and it did on many occasions.

I might not have had the best clothes, but my nan made me laugh so much. I think she was trying to cover up the bad stuff in my life with laughter. She felt bad because my mum and dad didn't want me. She would always say to my grandad, "Poor little sod, who wants him? No one." It wasn't their fault – they both worked, and other adults around me should have taken responsibility, but didn't.

Nan and Grandad were always at work. My nan's shop was just up the road from Greenwich swimming baths. I loved going swimming when I was younger, so I would go whenever I could. One time when I was about 10 or 11, just as I was going to go into the cubicle to get changed, one of the lifeguards that worked there, a man called Harry, said, "The changing rooms have moved. You're supposed to be downstairs." He said he would show me to the new changing rooms. They were empty at that time of night. Harry had his lifeguard's shorts on, but he ended up getting changed, even though he wasn't going swimming. He was just meant to be showing me where the rooms were.

He got a tape measure out and said, "Why don't you measure it?"

"Measure what?"

"Measure your willy."

"What do you mean? No, no, I don't want to do that."

I didn't have any hair down there. He held the tape measure against me and I pulled away. Then he did it to his. I didn't go swimming for a little while after that because it was quite freaky, and I wanted to avoid him.

But eventually I went back because I didn't want to miss any more swimming. I wanted to train and make sure I got the pass into swimming club for the following year. I always thought that swimming might be my way out of my shit life. Harry wasn't always there because the lifeguards worked shifts, but one of the other kids said to me, "Don't worry, he does that to me all the time."

I continued to go to the swimming baths, but no longer just to swim. By this time, I'd discovered a new hobby: arcade games. The swimming baths always had the latest games, so I spent hours playing Pac Land, Robocop and Galaxy. I would learn the patterns of the game, and got to know them so well that I could complete most of them on just one credit (10p).

Learning a computer's pattern at such an early age would prove a handy skill when I got older. All computers are built by a human, which means they must follow a pattern of some sort. Even computers that make financial decisions about us have a pattern. With an arcade game, if you find the pattern, you complete the game. If you find the pattern that a finance company has, you can hit the jackpot.

I never went near Harry after the episode in the changing

rooms. If I was round by the games, he would come up to me

and say, "I haven't seen you in a while, why don't you come swimming?" I'd say, "I've already been, and I'm waiting for my dad to pick me up." Then I shivered because I knew that no dad was coming to pick me up. There was nobody to call if the same thing happened again.

I met J while swimming one day. We raced, swimming up and down the length of the pool like we were Olympic athletes. After we got changed, J followed me down the road just past my nan's shop to Ozone's chippy. He said he wanted to get some chips as well. I became mates with him. He turned up most days I went swimming, always avoiding Harry, and we would do the same thing again, always with chips after. His Dad, Frank, seemed like a cool guy to me: he came to pick J up from the chippy, and always gave me 50p and a fag to smoke.

CHAPTER THREE

My First Scam

Greenwich is my manor. Five and a half miles south-east of Charing Cross, it is notable to outsiders for the National Maritime Museum, the Cutty Sark, the Royal Park, the University, and now the O2 Dome. The population is about 30,000, although until 1965 it was part of the London County area, and before that, Kent. Some of the old houses, like my nan's on Tyler Street, around the corner from Maize Hill Overground station, have quite a rustic look to them, because when they were built, this was still the countryside. But to me, Greenwich is a vast urban sprawl of council estates and barely reclaimed slums with tight social connections. If you're not from around here and you go in the wrong pub, it goes quiet and people will look at you to question why you're there, just like you see happen in those old westerns. They don't accept outsiders – not because they're unfriendly, but because there's moody stuff going on in most of those places. On a Saturday afternoon when the football's on, the toilets will be full of people having conversations with someone called Charlie. That's just how it is. On any council estate anywhere, there's hookie gear being sold. By the time we were 13, we were the ones flogging it.

On top of the arcade games, we had started to develop an interest in fruit machines and telephones, and all the money inside them. My friend Malcolm was the first one who showed me and my friend Salty how to do it. To play the arcade games at the swimming baths, we got a coin and pushed it up inside the return coin slot, spinning it up, and it would give us two credits instead of one. An olden-day glitch. Because he was a bit older than us, Malcolm knew all the scams – like going into the launderette, lifting the payphone, tapping the top, tapping the number, and it would connect a call. Malcolm was resourceful, and he shaped my brain a bit. He would go around and ask for work: "Got any pallets?" Back then you could get £1.50 for a pallet.

Sponsorship forms were how we first started scamming. Going door to door, we asked people to give us money for a sponsored skate, sponsored bounce, or sponsored run! A sponsored whatever it was – we'd take their money without doing anything. The trouble was, it wasn't scalable enough. We could only go to so many doors. Soon we were looking for other ways to make money.

I'd be out in October, just before bonfire night, trying to get "A Penny for the Guy" in quickly. Then as soon as 6 November came, I'd be out carol singing straight away. "We wish you a Merry Christmas…" I knew all the carols, because Christmas, to us, meant money. In the manor, I was known as a ruthless carol singer.

In the summer, I worked on the boating lake in Greenwich Park on and off until I was about 12 or 13, with a couple of other kids I met through Malcolm, for £1 an hour. We did seven hours on a Sunday, got £7 for it, went to KFC for £1.99, then had £5 left over for fags. That was 40 fags I could go into school with on a Monday morning and sell for 20p each, giving me £8 for two packs. Soon I had several different income streams. In the corporate world I work in today, they call it a sales funnel.

"Carding up" was something we did in phone boxes. We figured out that if we took a playing card and put it in above the return coin slot, when people went to use the payphone, they'd put in 50p to make a call, but they'd only use 20p, so 30p would be given in change. But when the coin dropped, it would get caught on top of the card, and we'd come to collect the change later. There are 52 cards in a deck, plus two jokers. That's 54 phone boxes that I could put all these cards in each day. We could get £3 a day off 10 phone boxes, but I did 50 at a time. We had worked out that one part of the machine was a weak spot, and upscaled it. It was a handy lesson in how to make quick money.

There were two big families in Greenwich: the Bleaches and the Pintos. The Pintos moved to the top of my road when I was about 10. Everybody who knew them loved them. The dad, John, was a car mechanic. Their mum, Mrs P, was always in the kitchen, cooking up the most colourful and delicious West Indian food, always with a big smile on her face, and greeting everyone who came to the door with a smile too. Their parties were legendary, with hundreds of people invited and nobody left out, from the churchgoers to the likes of us. They were, and still are, always willing to help others. It's always like that with people who come from council estates: everyone mucks in together and looks out for each other.

The daughter, Jennifer, started dating Dave Courtney, a debt collector who arranged Ronnie Kray's funeral, when I was a kid. Jennifer gave me my first pair of roller skates – Bauer quads – and I will always love her for that. Those skates gave me freedom. I could skate backwards, do the spread eagle, and give girls the tongue from between my legs as I zoomed past them.

We started a street hockey team called the South East Warriors, basically a mix of two teams: the Roller Warriors, whose best player was Mike, and us. Mike wanted to hang around with us now, as we had more fun than the other kids and he loved it.

We would spend all day playing on the wimpy asphalt, jumping off the cranes into the sand or stones, or playing war with our Gat guns, shooting each other with 1.77 pellets. One day we swam out to the barges, which were left out there while they were waiting to be filled with cargo. We sunbathed on them, diving in and out of the water. Then, after we had had our dinners, we all met up to put our skates on and go to play in the old flats. Dyson House, the estate where Del and Paul lived, led on to Glenthorne, which in turn led on to Chilver Street, where Jim Bobby lived.

All the kids from all the estates and hangout spots would meet up and play run-outs for hours. Then there were the Meridian flats just opposite my old school, just by the river. Loads more kids lived there: Joanne Hall, Scott and Kelly Sheppard, Andrew, and his uncles Terry and Tim. That was also where Malcolm and his brother Michael lived. There was a crazy black man called Winston, and every time we walked past his house, he would shout "Fuck Owff!" in his West Indian accent.

Then there was Lemmon Road, where Mike lived, and more kids that we hung around with occasionally. There was one kid, Jack Barclay, who was a few years older than me. He had an older brother, Jerry, and two sisters, Jess and Tina. Tina always used to run away when she heard a police siren, for some reason. Jack taught me how to steal car radios. Not many people liked him, because he was a bit of a bully if he didn't like you. He was only like that to me a couple of times. He was a racist though, towards Indian and Pakistani people. He would say, "Gord, blimey blimey" in a silly accent whenever he saw someone of that origin. It was clearly influenced by TV shows such as *Alf Garnett* and *It Ain't Half Hot Mum*.

So, we were a bunch of misfits. Del, Salty, Jim Bobby, Jess, Luke and Ellis joined forces with Mike and the Roller Warriors. We then went looking for a sponsor. It was Jim Bobby's idea. We went into ELS, a furniture superstore, and approached this guy called Pete. He told us that ELS wouldn't sponsor us, but he was willing to give us his time and train us. We did a sponsored skate to raise money to buy our kit – the first time we actually used the money we raised as we said we would!

We skated to Croydon. Pete from ELS became another father figure for me. I used to rely on him, though he let me down quite a bit. He'd tell me he would pick me up, but I'd stand waiting at the bottom of our road for hours and he wouldn't turn up. He had his own issues going on and wasn't concerned with mine, but when you're a kid, waiting around for hours, you're not interested in listening to their issues. I was excited because I thought I was going to drive around Southend seafront in his flash car and get a bit of attention from some girls.

There were plenty of times when he did show up, and we had fun. One of the first things he did was get us all in the back of an old Ford Transit van and take us on a night out to Roller City – a team-building exercise, he called it. There were about 15 of us all squashed up in the back, tools and blankets all over the floor belonging to whoever's van it was that Pete had borrowed. He gave his time, and I'll always give him credit for that.

Skating up and down Greenwich would bring us into contact with different girls from all the different estates. 15 fit 13-to-15-year-old boys skating around grabbed the attention of lots of them, and we loved it. There was one girl I fancied and used to follow around, showing off in front of her, trying to get her attention. She had been out with Jamie Mitchell, so why wouldn't she go out with me, I asked myself. I finally plucked up the courage to ask her out.

"Go away, you little tramp. I'd never go out with somebody like you," she said.

It was a huge rejection at the time, and I was crushed. I looked at my skates, the ones Jennifer gave me, and realised, if I was going to be accepted, I would need to transform myself. How was I going to change and become somebody else? It was my "cool rider" moment, and just like Michael from *Grease 2*, I decide to change my identity.

I have always known people only know what you tell them, and a wise man once said to me, "Believe nothing of what you hear and only half of what you see." Swagger comes from the way you carry yourself – it's not just about what you wear, it's how you walk, speak and conduct yourself. Swagger is one way of social engineering, and it plays a massive part in any con. But the art of social engineering is telling someone what they don't know, telling them something in a way that touches on emotion. By doing this you gain an opportunity, and it just comes down to what you use that opportunity for. Before I could use it for financial gain, I had to hone my skills.

The prettiest girl in town was called Sharon Cloud, the older sister of Jess, Luke and Ellis. She was drop-dead gorgeous. The Clouds would have parties now and then, and we could go as the boys' friends – not that any of us lot went for that. We just wanted a chance to speak to Sharon. We were just little boys fantasising over the hottest girl in the manor. She was older than me, but I saw that as a challenge. If I could manipulate her into kissing me – well, then I could do anything. So that's what I did. Sharon and I walked down to an off-licence at about 8 pm, after playing on the green, where I had been smoking.

"I'd never be able to kiss a girl as pretty as you," I said with a shy smile.

"Of course you would," she said, and she kissed me.

In my head, all I could think was *wow*. Maybe she thought I was dazed or something, but I was standing there thinking, *It worked!* Something just clicked when I said those words. I suddenly knew I could manipulate her into behaving how I wanted. I knew that would be her response. *Wow.*

That was just the first test, my first confidence trick. I would later realise how I could use emotion to tap into the psyche. For the first time, I was not using my physical body, violence, or speed to achieve what I wanted. I didn't need to. I was using feelings to get people to give me something. I didn't know it at the time, but I was social engineering.

CHAPTER FOUR

Robbing Lenny McLean

When I went to my secondary school, Eaglesfield, I learnt about Penny Up The Wall. It's a children's game where you all get 10p pieces, and whoever can toss them closest to the wall has the first spin. Then you get all the coins together, throw them up in the air, and say heads or tails. If five coins fall on heads, you get five coins. If one coin falls on heads, you get one. The more people play Penny Up The Wall, the more money you can make. So, I honed my skills at getting the penny close to the wall, because I wanted the money.

There was a kid I met in class called Darren Brennan. He was just like me, wayward as fuck, creating problems, beating up prefects, smoking in the toilet, eating crisps and chasing girls. He was exactly the type of kid I wanted to be around. Then there were two other kids who used to call me Gyppo because I wore a long sheepskin coat. I only lasted one year at that school: I got booted out for slapping a teacher after he called my nan thick. I grabbed his tie and slapped him. The school expelled me, and I had to go to a support centre in Eltham called Kings

Park. It was for the naughtiest kids around. You could only go there for six weeks and they would whip you into shape and get you back into the school system. Or so they thought.

After Kings Park I could apply for two new schools and one had to accept me. I put down John Roan, where all my mates from my area went, and Kidbrooke. They gave me Kidbrooke; John Roan had turned me down. Perhaps because my reputation had preceded me. I only lasted six weeks in Kidbrooke: I had countless fights and following my trial period, they refused me. The only option then was home tutoring with a woman called Mrs Ford. I had to go to her house every day, and she would teach me how to read and write. She set off my fascination with TV and film. I could do all the things that I had struggled with at school, because she took the time to teach me.

Dave Courtney used to train at a gym called Slim Jim's, above the Co-op in Greenwich, just around the corner from my old house and down the road from Jennifer Pinto's house. The notorious bare-knuckle fighter, Lennie McLean, trained there too. Going in through the side door and up the stairs, there were the training rooms, weights and punching bags, and a juice bar. Up another flight of stairs was the sauna and jacuzzi, and the men's changing rooms. There were no lockers or anything like that – blokes would just strip, get changed and leave their clothes hanging up.

It was about a pound to get in and do some weights at the gym. I'd watch them working out sometimes, but

Jonjo and Kenny, the two guys who ran the gym, didn't like me. "Little shit, go on, fuck off!" they'd say to me. They hated me. I was mouthy. "Come on, then!" I'd say, then I would run off, giving them the wanker signs. Laughing as they got close to me, before accelerating away. Big fucker, Jonjo was – you didn't want him catching you and giving you a clump.

I did get caught by one fat bloke one time though, when I had been nicking the sausages from O'Hagan's sausage shop. It was the world's first ever sausage shop. We would sneak in, get right up to the counter and steal the samples of sausages he left out for paying customers to try before they bought them. We also used to steal from the Indian man in the tandoori. We figured out that if you placed an order, they would go out the back and start cooking. They left no one in the front of the shop, so if you pushed the door slowly, the alarm that let them know someone was in the shop wouldn't go off. We could then jump up on the counter and lean over, open the till and nick the cash. One day he caught me, and he beat the shit out of me with a broom handle.

Guy Ritchie's films and the bare-knuckle documentaries hadn't come out yet, so I didn't even know who this Lenny McLean was. We got up the stairs in the gym and there were all these trousers, shoes, shirts and jackets in the room smelling like talcum powder and old spice.

I rubbed my mucky fingers inside those jackets and jeans, fumbling for crinkled paper. "Oh look, there's a £20 note in that one." The plan was not to take everything, because they'd know what had happened – whereas if they didn't realise, we could come back and do it again. But we weren't as smart as we thought we were.

When we got outside, Lenny was waiting by Star Burger. I don't know how he knew that was where we'd be. As soon as we got money, we would always go out straight away and spend it on food. Maybe he used to do the same thing when he was a kid. Anyway, we were brazen.

He was waiting, and as we came out, he shouted, "Oi! Come here." He grabbed me by the ears and picked me up. "Do you know who I fucking am?" he growled. "I'd rip Mike Tyson's fucking head off!"

He's a massive guy, with a huge head. He put me down and I said, "No you wouldn't, you fat cunt." And I bolted. He might have been a great fighter, but there was no way he would catch me.

I didn't know who Lenny was until years later. My cousin Tommy Cardwell had been in jail with him. Lenny was in for the 1992 Hippodrome case. He'd given some guy a backhander while working the door at a club. He was fitted up for manslaughter – and bust the case.

Everybody in the area knew Tommy Cardwell. Tommy and his best mate Danny Sadler were very naughty. I admired Tommy and Danny growing up. I'd be out late at night wandering around, and I'd see them staking out the shops they were about to burgle. I was learning the trade, figuring out what he was doing. Tommy was the first criminal to tell me, "You could go all the way. You've got the mind to be a super-criminal."

None of these guys were like some of the criminals of today. They would help an old lady cross the street, not rob them of their life savings! As much as people think there are no morals in the underworld, that just wasn't true where I came from. Mums and nans were held in the highest regard. They were the ones who looked after us as we were growing up, and they were the ones who could inflict the most pain on us too. So we did know right from wrong, but most of us were willing to go further than straight goers to get by.

I nicked my first car with Danny. We stole a Capri. He showed me how the clutch had a lock on it that attached to the steering wheel – one of the long ones that extended from the steering wheels to the pedals. If you lifted the clutch, you could take it off. *Wow!* I thought. *It's that easy?!* Because it had a steering lock on it, he grabbed it and told me to push and turn at the same time. It snapped, so we put a screwdriver in with a hammer and turned the ignition, and we were off, driving down Peckham High Street.

I was wicked at pinging windows and stealing car stereos. We figured out that if you got a spark plug and broke the ceramic bit around it, you could throw the chunk of ceramic at a car window, and it was like shooting a gun with a silencer. We just pushed the glass through, opened the door, and took the radio: Alpines, Sharps, Panasonics. People used to screw them in, because little fuckers like me would come along, ping the windows and nick the radio, equalisers and speakers.

All that stuff was valuable. This was Greenwich, so there was a never-ending supply of cars in the car parks.

Those car parks were great for making money. We would stand out there all day: "Wash your car for two quid, Mister?" Then, at night, we nicked their car stereos. Our whole childhood was about the next cash injection.

For us, though, nicking money was partly about eating. Part of our ritual after any scam was that we would always go and get a bit of food straight after. Music and food kept me focused.

I met one geezer in a kebab shop because I'd nicked a camera out of a car and we were selling it for 50 quid. The guy was going to buy it in the shop, and he said, "I'm looking for a car stereo."

"I can get you as many as you want," I said, dead cocky. "How much you want it for?"

"How much are they?"

"I can get you one for £80. It's worth £400. I've seen it. I know where it is. I'll get it for you."

I started there, delivering the goods to him the next night. Then he said, "My mate wants one as well, a Panasonic." So I got another one. One of my mates took that to an extreme, stealing hundreds of stereos. I would always steal to order – that was my business model, because I wanted to get rid and get paid on the same day. I didn't want to find places to store them, nor did I want the risk of getting caught with stolen goods. Plus, I was about the payoff. What was the point of keeping stock with no payoff?

By now it was quickly turning into a lifestyle, with all the rules and regulations about keeping things quiet, and the networks closed. But dealing in hookie gear meant that the phone line at my nan's could get quite busy at times. The phone would ring for me so much that the parrot, Big Bird, learned to imitate the ringing of the phone, and then my nan calling after me, "Tony, phone!" That bird fucking hated me.

Image is everything to some people. For me, it's okay to get in a piece-of-shit car and drive around, but if you want to get in the big-boy car, do it out of the manor: park it up and leave it somewhere else. Only let the manor see every now and then. Pretend you're driving for somebody.

But some people's egos need to be stroked too much. You can spot them a mile off, and because of this, they can be exploited to the max. When criminals get like this and want to show off their wares, they risk it all. Look what happened to the Great Train Robbers, and Henry Hill. One loose cannon in your team and you get caught. If you are up to criminality, you don't want the whole world to know about it. It's a secret. Let the ones who like to show off dig their own grave. The shadows are much safer for me.

CHAPTER FIVE

Computers Don't Commit Crime – People Do

My first computer crime was working out how to take films out for free at Ritz Video, delete videos off the system, and go back and get them. F9, F10, return, return.

The best machines were fruit machines – more patterns. They were everywhere when you knew where to look. They were full of cash, and in the 80s they were in all the caffs in Greenwich. As long as you bought something in the cafe, the owner would let you play the machine, so in the morning before school, we'd go to the caff, get a coffee, and play the machines. We wouldn't just randomly go to the cafes, though. We would pick the perfect times to play.

At 7:30 am we would be at the Wagon Wheel. 8 am would be Guzzles. Then round to Charlie's for 8.30 am. If we missed the time slot for one of the machines – normally because Del was still doing his hair – we could tell if it had already paid out. It was like the machine would be upset that it had just emptied its guts of cash. To test it, we would put 10p in the slot. If the reels spun really fast, that meant we were too late for that one and there was no point in playing on, so we would just move on to the next caff.

There was one machine they had in the Chinese shop, a pressure game where you pressed the button and the lights moved up past different fruits, depending on how much pressure you applied to the button. Get five cherries in a row and you won a pound, get five melons in a row and you won a fiver. I waited until people had been playing it all day, filling up all the rows of fruits. I'd come straight in and ping it for a fiver on my first go. Then the lemons for another £4, oranges £3, and so on. Most days I'd leave the Chinese shop with £12 – not bad for five minutes' work.

These fruit machines were run by the likes of Freddie Foreman, Frankie Fraser and the Richardson gang. They installed their machines in caffs, restaurants and bars all over south London, and in exchange they protected the little guys from other criminal gangs that would rob the collection drivers of their cash. So, in effect, we were stealing from other, much more dangerous criminals. It wouldn't be the last time, and I wouldn't find that out until many years later.

There were a couple of ways of properly doing fruit machines though. The first required a wire from a garden strimmer. I made a hook on the end of the wire, stuck it down the coin slot, hooked the little metal arm and pulled, to clock up credits. We fooled the machine into believing we were putting money in – again, it was just a pattern really, giving the machine what it believed to be correct. A machine can only do what a human has programmed it to do.

Then, just like all criminals do, we figured out a much quicker way to manage it. We watched one of the engineers pull the front glass forward and fiddle with something, and the money just ejected. We worked out what it was he pressed, got a solid metal rod and cracked the metal edge. We pulled the glass forward, stuck our hand down, pressed the button, and all the money ejected. But that was only the payout, and people always put more in than they got out, so the real money was in the bottom. That part was only made of wood, so we figured that if you booted it in the right place, you could stick your hand through and get all the pound coins.

That was the first thing we did properly as a team. I'd started going out with a girl I'd met hanging around by the Cutty Sark, and you might say she was also my first inside informant. Her name was Kim, and she worked at London Arena. She said, "Come over for the day and bring your mates – I'll get you in for free and get you all some burgers." They had Timmy Mallett and other kids' shows being filmed there.

They had a purpose-built hockey pitch in the middle of it that we used to train and play in. It was run by Patrick Power, whose son is now a famous grime producer called Jamma. Jamma played hockey for his team, the Hurricane All Stars. At the end of the summer holiday, they took it all down and built a fairground. It had rides inside, as well as loads of arcade and fruit machines. It wasn't like the guys who did travelling fairs, it wasn't show people – it was the corporate fairground. They didn't know what we could do, and they were vulnerable. They had all these arcade machines, but we were there specifically for the fruit machines. There were five of us tooled up, and we destroyed them.

It was me, Mack, Del, Salty, and Martin Rock. We had hockey bags and we skated there in the evening. In each fruit machine there was maybe £200, so five machines was a grand. It didn't take long – a matter of seconds and we were in. There were whole rooms without any arcade games, just fruit machines flashing and making the most mental sounds. We had little bags, clear plastic ones from the bank, and we filled them up. It was a real operation. Nobody suspected anything, because there was so much noise and music, flashing lights, so much distraction – and very little security to be seen. We had hidden our hockey bags behind the burger counter where Kim worked, so when the job was done we went back to them, put the money in the bags, put our skates on and skated back with all the money weighing us down.

We arrived back to one of the caffs called The Wagon, on the same parade as my nan's shop, tired. We got some food and then we counted the money out and carved it up. We had got thousands. £16,000 in fact – about three grand each.

It took forever to get rid of those pound coins. I wasn't exactly going to take them to the bank to get them changed to notes. But I was still transforming, creating

44

my own cool rider, so I bought Nike Airs and Reebok tracksuits from Champion, which I'd never been able to have before. I bought a Chippy jacket, reversible denim, that cost £125. That set us on our way. It gave us money to get the same things as the other kids.

That clobber gave me confidence. I was no longer a little tramp. It made finding girls a bit easier. But I didn't tell my nan or anybody else. They had no idea. If they saw me wearing it, so what? I worked seven hours on the boating lake! I'd always had a job. Understanding how I looked on the outside was pragmatic – I needed to be able to cover myself. But people only knew what I told them.

I wasn't conscious of the direction my life was heading in. I didn't have any thoughts about my trajectory. I was just a kid going along with life.

Then one of the kids went and robbed a shop. He nicked a load of shoes and flip-flops, and went door to door selling them. Everyone on the estates bought stuff from him.

I was enjoying spending money, but it was playing on my mind that the arcades didn't come around very often. Try doing it at a fairground, and they'll catch you and beat the shit out of you. That London Arena heist was what I'd call a criminal opportunity. My whole team understood that opportunity and took it, obliterated it. We needed more of them.

Del and I were grafting, one day, breaking into a shed. We spent the whole day chipping a lock out, going all round it with a chisel – chip, chip, chip – to nick a Honda

C90 motorbike, only to crash it up the road and nearly decapitate ourselves. But we were living how we wanted to live. We had a room where we'd sit and congregate; we'd take girls there of a night, when we were 14 or 15, meeting kids from all over the place: Deptford, Catford, Lewisham, Plumstead, Abbey Wood. Hanging about at the Cutty Sark, we were 50 strong.

We'd be sitting around smoking – maybe a bit of puff – drinking a little bit, maybe. At the time, "youths" and "antisocial behaviour" were becoming an issue for the media and politicians. We moved from place to place, bothering people sitting outside Greenwich District Hospital, where I was born. Before, you'd just get pissheads sitting outside the Accident and Emergency, but then we all started congregating there. That was where I met one of the older boys, Stuart Toal, and became instantly fascinated.

Stuart didn't like me because I was nosy. I'd heard he was a wicked car thief and I wanted to up my game, so whenever I saw him, I would ask questions: how do you do this, and how do you do that? I tried to find out all the tricks of his trade. I wanted to hang out with him and dress like him, in the latest C17 jeans, Fila, and Reebok Classics hi-tops. Stuart was four years older – I was 14 and he was 18 – and that was a big jump, because he'd already been to jail and got a bad-boy name around the manor. Everyone called him Smoothie because he was a tidy footballer and a good-looking bloke.

His house was one of those 1980s buildings in between a load of Victorian terraces. When I knocked for him, his Mum opened the door. "Go on, go up." I went up the stairs to his room. I could hear music. As I walked in, Stuart had a broom handle stuck in his drawer like a microphone, with another broom in his hand, singing Dire Straits into the mic. I remember watching him and thinking, *How cool is that!* I wanted to be around him. He saw me and yelled, "What the fuck you doing? You little cunt!" and started going mad.

Later that day he took me to Charlton – the Cardwell estate – and I saw a different kind of criminality. It wasn't a "gang", because gangs didn't really exist like the media might have you believe – it was just a load of kids in a council estate in the middle of Charlton with nothing better to do. But they were making money. Stealing cars to order and nicking anything that wasn't nailed down.

That was when I learned to split into two people. I was able to adapt to that part, and still go home to my nan, getting along with the old dears in the salon who didn't understand this new urban street culture.

Canary Wharf was going up on the northern bank of the Thames, and I was looking at it thinking, *Things can only get better.* I read the *Sun* because it was the common paper, but I didn't understand any of the landscape and how it interacted with finance. I didn't know what shares were, or markets. But as a kid who grew up building camps on the hill next to the station and the pub we'd looted – we'd smoke puff and take girls there – I understood that the most wood made the best roof. Looking across the river and seeing how many cranes there were, I saw the bright lights of the future within touching distance, and I wanted to touch them all.

Soon Stuart asked me, "Do you want to come and steal some wheels with me?"

Stuart stole cars, and we stole the wheels off cars. We would break into garages by smashing the asbestos roof and dropping inside. Jack the car up and steal the wheels. Stuart stole a double-decker bus once, a number 180. He drove along the route with the hat on and picked people up. People loved him for it. Then he nicked a police car and they nabbed him. They had him handcuffed, but he still got away. He went to jail at Feltham and got three years for TDA – Taking and Driving Away. It's called TWOC now – Taking Without Consent. That lot got into commercial burglaries, and you learn things from burglaries, like how to break a window properly, or how to talk your way into somewhere, leave a window open, and come back at night to rob the place. These were the tricks of the trade.

I and my mates linked up with my cousin Jo and some of the girls from her children's home. Jo had come to live with us when she was in her early teens. She had had a troubled upbringing. After a few months of living with us, Jo was taken away to a children's home. She was only allowed to come and stay with us at weekends. But this meant that each weekend we had a pack of rebellious girls and boys, all trying to impress one another with how bad they could be, hanging around the streets of Greenwich causing all sorts of anti-social behaviour.

Del and I would nick bikes. I'd take a BMX, spray it, and change little bits. One of my mates, Peter Thorn, cut bikes in half and connected one to another. He was a real don at making bikes, and he had a PK ripper. I had loads of BMXs – about 100 in the outside shed – all in parts, ringed, with the numbers filed down. I kept chains and other parts in the front garden. For a while, all my focus was on bikes. Nan just saw it as "doing bits and pieces." She didn't ask any questions; most boys were doing stuff like that. My nan and grandad were at work, so they didn't know what was going on outside the house. I think they always just told themselves I was a hard worker – I had a legitimate job in her shop or washing cars or on Greenwich boating lake. I was good at hiding what I was up to.

The only times I caught any heat was for stealing from the sweet shop when I was eight or nine – the owner called the police, but couldn't prosecute me. I was way below the age of criminal responsibility, so I just got a telling off. Then later, in my teens, when Del had been stopped riding his bike, it was him and Big Bird who almost gave me away.

Del had nicked a bike off a dead bloke's balcony after another Mission Impossible heist, when he got stopped by the Old Bill. He told them that he had paid the guy for the bike before he died. When they asked if there was anyone that could verify his story, he gave my name. The Old Bill showed up at my nan's house, and of course, she wouldn't let them in.

"Where's Tony?" they asked.

"He's out," my nan replied. On this occasion, it happened to be true. Nan was very house-proud, though, and she would have fought them off before they were allowed to come stomping in all over her carpets, turning over her antiques, or going through her prized possession: the globe drinks bar.

While my nan was fending off the Old Bill at the front door, Big Bird was in the living room doing his nut in. "Tony, phone! Tony, phone!"

The Old Bill ended up finding all the bike ringing gear, but because all the numbers had been filed off, there wasn't any evidence to prove they'd been nicked. They didn't put two and two together, luckily for me – because Big Bird might have been able to tell them something.

"Tony, phone!"

"Who is it?" they might have asked.

"Some bloke asking if you can get him a fixed-gear Raleigh, or a new car stereo."

That taught me a very valuable lesson, though: don't shit where you live.

CHAPTER SIX

Revenge

There was one thing I was desperate to take care of in my personal life, and that was how to get back at bad John, my ex-stepfather who used to hit my mum. I knew where he lived because he was still in the same place where he had shacked up with my mum as a kid, just behind my primary school. I used to see him around the shops, his dirty grey form carrying plastic bags.

With the money that I'd made from selling stereos and bikes, I bought a baseball bat. It was a red wooden baseball bat, a Wilson. I loved that bat.

I blamed John for destroying my mum's relationship with me, for beating her up and destroying my nan: she was so upset whenever she saw how her daughter had been beaten up. I couldn't wipe the memories from my mind. Beater Basher had said to me, *When you get to 15, when you think you're a man and you're big enough, we'll have a go.*

After one of the beatings he gave my mum I tried to intervene and save her, but I was a kid and my efforts were futile.

51

I thought, *I'm big enough now. I've got this weapon and I'm willing to use it.*

I watched him for about 15 days. Some days he would go to the supermarket, and others he would go to the little shop. Some days he would go to the Post Office, others he wouldn't go anywhere. Some days he would go to the pub, and others, back to the supermarket. I was gathering intel about him, learning his patterns. I wanted to wait until he had bags in his hands. I thought, *I'm going to do to you what you did to her. How dare you think that you can do what you did to her? How dare you? Do you think you can hurt my Mum?*

He came out of the supermarket with his bags, and he got on a bus.

I had the bat in the back of my tracksuit bottoms, with my collar turned up. He didn't recognise me anymore, because I was a man.

He got off the bus, and walked past my old school. There was a little alleyway he had to walk through. I waited in the alley… Took the bat out…

My mate told me always to do it with two hands, because you'll get a vibration. When you hit something, you'll hear a crack, but it takes all the stress out.

I could feel the wind rushing past my face. I was there, in the present, as this scumbag was drudging past. He passed the houses, then the gate, then the school. I waited with the bat around my neck, ready to swing. As he came past, he didn't see me. I swung it at his fucking head and cracked him on the back of the skull. He went down in a heap, and I walked away.

I'm a man now!

After Beater Basher, I knew I would be willing to use violence if needed. I knew my capabilities. I had learned what I was willing to do. The feeling I would get from it. And the feelings certainly weren't all good. I was worried: *Is he dead, is he not dead?* I was probably also worried about the backlash if he was – going to prison for life. But by the time I got to the bottom of the road, he'd got up. But the way I'd done him was lovely. He didn't know what had hit him. He was properly dazed. Staggering, leaning against the wall. I carried on watching him in that slow agony, until he was on his hands and knees, crawling.

I saw him two weeks later with a bandage over his head, his face all fucked from where he must have fallen. Good. That was how my Mum must have felt. He had battered my mum so much that he left her in the emergency room at the hospital, with broken ribs and a head swollen like a melon. He was lucky I didn't take the bat and iron him out properly. *Now you can have that to live with. I hope that's woken your brain up a bit, you woman beating piece of shit.* He might have gone to the Old Bill, but I didn't care.

Despite the fact that I believe people can change, he had committed so many wrongs against the people I love, that punishing him was the only thing which could give me some peace. I know what I did isn't right by society's standards but I don't feel any remorse.

CHAPTER SEVEN

Monty

At 14 I met Monty. He was a geezer from the area who smoked dope and did a bit of dipping – pickpocketing. He was a white guy with a bald head and his hair round the sides slicked back, and he had a greyish, straggly beard. With his blue mackintosh, he was a bit dishevelled round the edges, like most con guys. A bit like Fagin in *Oliver Twist*, he always had kids around him. My cousin Jo introduced me to him – he used to give him drugs, fuelling what later turned into a heroin addiction. One day I went around to Monty's flat in Sam Manors to buy some puff for £7.50.

Monty worked for Radio Rentals. To get a TV on rental, you had to go in and fill out a form stating your name, address, date of birth, occupation, and how much you could afford. You didn't need any photo ID, just a utility bill, and they'd tell you to come back and pick it up on Friday. Then you took your agreement into a store – not always the same branch – to pick up the TV or VCR. I washed the cars of people who worked there, including Monty. Once I was finished, I would go into the office to give them back their keys. I soon realised that there were no padlocks on the drawers. So when I was alone, I would help myself to the agreement forms and pass them onto Monty. He fitted them up with fake utility bills, and made off with a load of their equipment.

This was the first time I had seen pieces of paper – just A4 paper – turned into goods, and those goods, in turn, changed into cash. In the criminal world, that's what it's all about: the money. And with the upbringing I had, money seemed like the solution to all of life's problems.

Coming out of Monty's one day, I met somebody called T, and he showed me a new trick. He taught me about track two information: the information stored in the little black magnetic strip on the back of a credit card. For £30 he was giving Monty cloned credit card numbers, and I'd go out to a shop where one of us knew the owner. I'd spend £300 and we'd split the cash. I had a friend whose dad owned a restaurant, and he would let us in; his dad would swipe the card and give us back half of whatever it was that we swiped through. The cards were not even fake ones – just Argos Premier Points cards, with no signature strip.

T and his boys were Algerian, and some smart fucker realised that at the hotels in Algeria, the magnetic strip on their key cards was exactly the same as a credit card. To create key cards for rooms, hotels used a piece of equipment to read the information on those cards – room numbers and door codes, in this case – and programmed new numbers onto it. For hotels, it was a much better system than having physical keys, which required a lock-smith. With a digital system, all they had to do was press a button and programme a new card with a code. But that code wasn't limited to being a room number or a door code. On the "tracks" where the information was stored, you could add a credit card number and an expiry date. So, with one of these machines, you could turn any hotel room key, or any other card with a magnetic strip on it, into a replica of any credit or debit card.

T and I left Monty's at the same time. We walked along the road, until T suddenly stopped outside Star Burger on the corner. "Monty's telling me what you're doing," he said, "because he's getting the cards off me. Why don't you get them off me direct, and you'll make more money?" Monty's loose lips definitely sank his ship, because very quickly I cut him out of the deal and moved on to deal with T.

T lived in a pokey little flat at the other end of Greenwich. If these guys were committing high-level fraud, thousands per week, why weren't they living somewhere really nice? They probably were. Criminals need a base where they can deal with people – it might not be where they actually live. Although it still took him a while to take me there, we'd often meet on the street, outside Star Burger, and he'd turn up in an old Vauxhall Nova.

For my first transaction, I gave him £300 for 10 cards. I made £3,000 off them, going to shops where I knew the owners or the managers, swiping through a transaction and splitting the cash.

I put £2,000 away and bought another thousand's worth. They lasted me three weeks, and I made about £15,000.

For the next hit, I gave him £3,000 and he gave me something like 500 cards. That was the last time I shelled out for his cards. I wanted to cut him out of the equation too, just like I had cut out Monty, and start mining the numbers myself. It was time to invest in my first piece of computer equipment.

T had somebody working in a hotel, using the room key software to grab customers' credit card numbers. The guy brought these numbers back to T, and T would put them into a database on his computer and use the same machine to make his own replica credit cards.

Until then, the machine to clone a card had to be connected to a computer. Then T splashed out on a new wireless grabber, so he didn't need to be connected to a concierge's desk. Now he could take it anywhere. Waiters, shop assistants – anyone could keep this in their pockets and swipe a card, cloning it without the customer noticing. It was like a big USB stick with a slit at the side, which held the track two information on it when a card was swiped through.

I was sitting in T's living room smoking a fag while my team, Man United, was playing. I saw the wireless grabber sitting on the side in his little pokey flat, and decide to ask him about it. "Where did you get that from?"

T was cagey because he was making a nice little earner selling the card numbers to me. He turned to me and said, "You've got to go to Canada to get it. They're seven grand. You're better off buying them from me, it's easier that way." I found the same one for £3.5k in a trade magazine I found at the newsagent. I ordered it and got it delivered to my nan's address.

CHAPTER EIGHT

Building a Team

I had my grabber, but now I needed some insiders in shops and restaurants to steal credit card details for me. I've always had a knack for finding out what people want. I like to cut straight to the chase. If you keep messing around on the outside and not ever saying it to somebody, you don't know. But if you ask somebody, "Do you want to make some money?" Most people are going to ask, "How?" Then I say, "Look, how much do you earn a week? 200 quid maximum. What if I can make you an extra £300 a week on top of your wages?"

At first, a kid saying this to somebody may seem strange. But I wasn't just a normal kid. I was dressed well, and I had money and equipment. I could offer to swipe a card on the spot to prove it worked. I knew that most people, especially kids earning minimum wage, being spoken to like pieces of shit, would say yes to me. Why wouldn't they want to steal? They had no respect for the boss or the job. Most of the people they took money from treated them like they were worthless. Instead of spitting on the food, why wouldn't they get their own back by nicking their credit card details, and rinse them for a new wardrobe or even some nice diamond earrings? I spun it as a way of getting back at their customers.

In Greenwich, there was a youth club called 302, a big dance hall with a red canopy and black front, and wooden floors that were sticky and bouncy. The DJ would play "Snap", 1990s pop music, and they had a smoking area and bar. My lot weren't drinkers, but there would be kids getting drunk at the disco. Del and my mates were collaborating on little earners, sharing information and techniques, although our number one interest was girls.

At 302 I met Eve, a grunge girl who worked in a deli in Covent Garden. I gave my first wireless grabber to her, and she did more numbers in one day than T had told me they could get. She doesn't have to keep the grabber connected or close to the till: it was in her hand, so she could swipe every customer if she wanted to. T had only ever got 50 to 60 numbers per day with his. But Eve was in a busy deli, taking card payment after card payment. She was well-positioned, and because of this she got over 100 numbers on her very first day.

I went back to T so we could input them into his computer. He was stunned at how many credit card numbers she had grabbed. It was all about having the right people, in the right places, at the right time. The criminal opportunity. And I had a knack of always finding that sweet spot.

Word got around the streets and the youth club quickly that I could hook people up with these magic little computers that could double your wages. I didn't just have kids from the youth club, I also had older people coming to me, asking for a piece of the action, and I loved all the attention it brought me. I felt important.

One day Eve's boss caught her grabbing numbers in the deli at Covent Garden, and he called the Old Bill on her. She said some guy had offered her money in a pub to clone cards, and she was going to meet him in the same pub on Friday to give him the grabber back and collect her 300 quid. The Old Bill believed her and set up a sting to catch me, but there was nobody there. I'd given her a cover story, as I was aware of the links back to me and what could happen. She was a good girl and played it perfectly.

Although I was orchestrating a substantial crime wave, in retrospect this was just training: I was figuring out how to control a network and make people work for me. Initially, the cards we were using didn't look that legit. Salty knew somebody who got blank imitations, but they were terrible. The old-school forgers used to scan the front image into a computer and print a faded image with the MasterCard logo, but the long number on the front wasn't raised or embossed. It didn't take a security expert to tell those cards weren't legit.

Then he found somebody who could punch them up to give you a raised long card number. But on close inspection, they still weren't very convincing. Often the number would be slanted, or it would have been pressed too hard in the machine, giving it a distinctly homemade look.

The way I looked at it, this was becoming a business. Not only did I want it to work, but I also wanted to stay out of jail. So, I made enquiries and bought an embosser myself – from my guy T. Still smarting a bit from me cutting him out with my own grabber, he charged me £700 for something that was only worth £400. I didn't store it at my nan's: I paid somebody £50 a week to keep it in a cupboard in their flat. They didn't know what was in there, all in laundry bags stacked up: the beginnings of a crime empire!

At 16 I had money; I had a crash pad too, and an ever-expanding network of around 100 waitresses and barmaids cloning cards for me around London, and about 50 shop owners who'd swipe them through for cash. I set up a workshop where I was knocking out counterfeit credit cards that looked convincing, and I was using them to buy goods from every kind of store imaginable. I was getting clobber for myself and stealing to order for others: anything from groceries to trainers to big TVs. We still didn't have mobile phones, but I had a pager. And, of course, the landline.

I'd bought a car off Jamie Mitchell for £150, a beige Ford Cortina, and we sort of learned to drive it. All my mates did before we smashed it up. I was seeing the girl in Ritz Video, who taught me how to drive properly – and how to joyride properly. Her mum had a Saab, and she'd take us down the Asda car park and let us spin it around. We were enjoying the fruits of our labours, buying things that we didn't have.

We met some girls who lived in the private estate in Blackheath. One of the girls' dad had a Sierra, an old 1.8 white one, and she said, "This weekend you can drive it to the club if you want, and we'll all go together."

We went to Langtree's in Beckenham. It was an amazing place, everybody drinking snakebite and black, and getting pissed up. It was the first time I realised that alcohol makes you relax and that you could enjoy yourself. Not to excess like my mum and uncle – that just led to violence. My mum was only 17 years older than me. I'd seen her arguing and fighting with my uncle. I'd seen my mum lie in front of the fire and burn herself, because she was so drunk that she couldn't wake up. Still, I really enjoyed the atmosphere in the club, lipsing up girls just like I'd learned in the 302.

CHAPTER NINE

The Job Interview

Geoff was the dad of one of the skaters. When Pete left, he took over as team manager. Just like Pete, he realised I was quite intelligent. I wasn't asking for money, and he spotted that. Everyone thought I'd dropped out of school and was a proper thicko, but I was always the one who got up in the morning, knocking on my mates' doors, driving all that activity, because that's the kind of person I was.

One of the many things my nan taught me was "The early bird catches the worm." Even to this day, I am up most mornings at 4 am. Geoff could see that attribute though, he could see my leadership qualities, that my brain was sharpening differently from the other kids in the area.

Geoff taught me about becoming a man. He told me I was not going to stay in Greenwich for the rest of my life. He could see I had ambition. That sparked something off in my head. I wanted to move away from Greenwich, reinvent myself again.

Around that time, my dad had appeared back on the scene. He might be an arrogant wanker at times, but he was super intelligent, and a successful businessman in his own right. He was a litho man with big ambitions. His printers' company would do big Hollywood film posters and the leaflets that went out with their releases. He owned a factory in King's Cross, and that was where I saw my first printer.

My nan must have spotted I was up to something, because all of a sudden she started to hound me to get a job. Perhaps it was because she had found my stack of cash, hidden under my bed, or my new shiny grabbers. She questioned me: "Where did all that money come from?"

Instantly I replied, "I'm good at saving, Nan! One day I am going to give us all a different life."

A couple of days later she sat me down and said, "Ask your father if he has any jobs. He hasn't done fuck all for you. You need to be working, son, nothing good can come from bad money."

So, just to keep her happy, I asked my dad for a job.

I was 16 and a half. This was my first attempt to be normal, not just to use a job as cover for my nan. When I asked him, my dad said, "Yes, you can have a job, but you will need to have an interview with your uncle Lee". Lee was his partner in the business. So, on a Monday morning, I cycled from Greenwich to King's Cross. I arrived at 8.05 am, a little bit late. The first thing my uncle said was, "You need a haircut, and you're late." My uncle was really slick – perfect hair, no kids, caught up in his yuppie lifestyle – the perfect corporate man.

That interview taught me lessons at that age that I couldn't buy today. "You look like a mess," he said. "What kind of life can you expect if you look like that? You're going to amount to nothing."

I'm thick-skinned, and they couldn't deny me the job, but they wanted to put me through the rigmarole, to teach me a lesson. Maybe my nan had said something to my dad about the cash and equipment she had found in my room?

They showed me the ropes. It was the early days of litho printing: using graphics to print was a new format. I got to use the guillotine, and that was really interesting because it taught me about edges, how to get paper really sharp – knowledge I would use to my advantage years later. Later in life, I would be able to make utility bills so good they had the perforated payment slip on them. I even had the stamp that said "paid" on it – the one they used in the post office when you went to pay a bill. It was the perfect way to forge a document.

Around that time, I opened my first of many bank accounts at Barclays. I couldn't keep cash under my bed forever. The account came with a cheque book. There were no credit checks or anything back then. Banking was becoming retail, so they wanted people to open accounts. I was an inquisitive kid, so I'd go in and ask questions. I was social engineering. Finding out all the inside knowledge from the bank's staff.

I wanted to understand how the banking system worked, asking a question that would get me answers to guarded information – inside knowledge – but being smart in my questioning, just like the psychiatrists had been with me as a kid. Why did some cards go to authorisation and some didn't? I would find out as much information as I could – just banking knowledge, in case this new job didn't work out.

One time I asked about how cheques were verified by shops. "Transax," came the reply. Because so many people around the world were now committing cheque fraud, this was the new system they had brought in: a traffic-light system for fraud detection and prevention. It could spot a dodgy cheque, or if you didn't have enough funds in your account. Green for yes, amber for maybe, and red for a definite no.

One of the clerks told me that as long as you had money in your account and stayed under that amount, the cheques would always clear, no matter how many you wrote, so you could cash as many as you wanted as long as you did it before the first cheque cleared. Six months later, I jacked in the job at my dad's, and kicked back for a little bit. He was paying me £25 a day, and that was never going to get me anywhere.

CHAPTER TEN

Sweet Seventeen

On 17 January 1991 the first airstrikes took place on Iraq. It was watching it on the news, but then switched over to a programme that would change my life forever. It was a BBC programme all about voting. While everyone else was watching the missiles land on Baghdad and worrying about World War Three, I was figuring out more ways to commit crime. I was still smashing cloned cards: by this time my network had grown to over 300. People were either working for me or working for someone using my stuff. TV would also teach me about the boom in finance and the rising debt the UK that the world was plummeting into. The show on the BBC showed how people's information was stored in libraries and on the electoral roll.

I went shopping in Topman on Oxford Street with some cloned cards. I was walking around picking stuff up to go and pay when I spotted a sign: "Buy now, pay 12 months later". It was the first time I saw it and thought, how about "Buy now, pay never"?

I approached the girl at the counter. "What does that sign mean?"

"You can get up to a thousand pounds to spend in store now."

"Wow! How does that work?" I asked.

"You need your bank card, name, address, date of birth, and something with your signature. I'll process it and if your application is successful you will get up to one thousand pounds to spend now."

I had bank cards on me, but I didn't have any addresses or bank details that I would need to open up the store card. I paid for the stuff I'd picked up with the moody cards, left the store and made my way home. All I could think about on the way back was getting one of those store cards. My brain was trying to find the pattern to hit the jackpot!

As well as making cards, we had been adding the track two information to real cards. That was the first time we used what they now call mules. A mule is someone who will permit you to use their information, bank account or credit card. They get paid for letting us use them. Nowadays, thanks to the internet, mules can be unsuspecting, but back then they all got paid for assisting us with our fraudulent behaviour. We would pay them to use their cards. We only needed the back of the cards for the magnetic strip. It didn't matter what names were on the front, as no one ever checked.

The people in the store were not going to check the card like that. If we were just paying on the card, they would just look at the signature strip on the back, compare it to what we had signed, and say, "Thank you, sir, have a nice day!" But for this job, they would need to look at the front of the card to check the name, and write the 16-digit number down from the front of the card on the application. They would also check the signature, but that was easy to sort out.

There are many ways to remove a signature from the back of a credit or debit card. Bleach and brake fluid are most fraudsters' choice. Mine was hairspray, though, and thanks to my nan's shop there was always plenty of that about. I could never understand all these old guys taking ages, dipping their little paint brushes in bleach. Using hairspray was like using a jet washer: all the ink would just wash off the back of the card. I could do 10 cards while the old boys were still messing about with the first one.

It was always better to hit the big stores. They had endless transactions going on: if a few moody ones slipped through, they wouldn't notice it. Big retailers, banks, bars and restaurant chains allowed for loss: customers sometimes paid 15% more for stuff because the shop factored all the losses in.

The only card I had in date said Mr P Patel on it. *Fuck! What am I going to do?* I had an idea. I went to the library and found a Mr P Patel. I took all my own work information from one of my previous Saturday jobs, and attributed it to him. I got some bank details from somewhere – just supplying any account number and sort code, because they could not check that they matched back.

The next day, I went back to the store on Oxford Street. I walked straight over to the girl I'd seen the day before. I told her I would like to open a store card, so she gave me a form to fill out. I'd spent ages trying to remember all the information about Mr Patel, expecting her to ask me all sorts of questions, but she gave me a form so I could turn around and scribble on my knee, simply copying over his details from the piece of paper where I had all his information written out. I filled it in and handed it over to her. She looked at the form, then at me again: "You don't look like a Mr Patel, sir."

"It's *Par-tel*," I said in a French accent. "It's not Indian, it's French!"

She went red. "I'm ever so sorry, sir." And she approved my store card.

That was the first time I knew how much the limit of a card was. They gave me a grand, and I promptly spent it. I bought a pinstripe gangster suit. I thought I was the dog's bollocks, although in that suit I probably looked like a right ball bag!

The following week, Mr Patel would get a letter through saying he'd opened up a store card on Oxford Street, and he would receive a statement from the finance company. These letters had a phone number on it for him to call if he had any problems with his account. I thought, *When he gets that letter, he'll tell them he didn't go to Topman, no harm done.* I had just committed my first identity theft. Up to that point I had spent most of my life wanting to be someone else – and now I could be. I was making a fortune from cloning cards, but what I

71

needed was more than money. The feeling it gave me was like being a secret agent. Only I knew who I really was. It was a rush.

Fraud is all about what you can convince people of in the here and now. After everything I had been through until that point in my life, it felt like I was born for that moment: I could be anyone. It was social engineering. In the movie *Catch Me If You Can*, Leonardo DiCaprio does it when he is playing Frank Abagnale in the bank scene. When he's eyeing up the teller, it's all in the instinct; he reads that person, creating an aura of confidence. Although Frank was finished with crime at 16 and locked up, I was just getting started.

By the time all the paperwork had arrived on Mr Patel's doormat, I was long gone, but looking extremely dapper in the suit that didn't cost a thing. Buy Now, Pay Never! At this point in my life, I wasn't even thinking about poor Mr Patel, whose credit file and life I had just ruined. For ever more, Mr Patel would have to jump through hoops to prove who he was. But as far as I was concerned, this was a victimless crime.

CHAPTER ELEVEN

Moving Out of Greenwich

I met a girl called Tara at Ritzy nightclub in Streatham. She was 19 and I was 17. She had a cheeky little smile. In clubs, we would just walk around until we spotted some girls we liked, and then just plot up. One of us would then go in, depending on who spotted them. On this occasion, it was my turn. My chat up lines back then were a bit cheesy.

"Alright luv, you come here often?"

She looked at me and said, "How old are you?"

I was always tall and looked older than my age, so I said I was 18.

"You look about 12," she said.

I didn't know what to say – I was standing there going all red-faced – but then she told me to get her a vodka and coke. So I did.

At the end of the night I walked her to her car, she gave me her number, and then she kissed me. She said she would like to see me again. The following Wednesday, I called Tara and we arranged to go out for a drink. I liked her. She was brash, bolshie and very cocky too. We started going out and before we knew it, I had moved out of my nan's place and moved in with her. Tara worked in Barclays, but got laid off, although she was a straight goer. I learned a lot because she worked in a bank, though – things like how to apply for credit cards and mortgages.

I wanted to move out of Greenwich and try to be normal. At 17 years old, I wanted to get away from crime. Meeting Tara seemed like that opportunity. Her dad Bernie had always been a smart person with money. They always used the financial system to their benefit. I had a credit card and store cards in my name and was paying them all off, learning more about how the systems worked. I discovered that if you had a problem paying the bill, you could ring up and negotiate.

If you got approved, you knew you had a good profile. For instance, if you had £2,000 to spend, you knew that "profile" – whether it was yours or somebody else's – had a good credit score. They didn't just dish out £2,000 to anyone for a starting limit. So, you could spend up to your limit and then call them up. "I know I've spent up to my limit, but the reason I got that card is because I really love the sofa that's in there, and it's £3,500. I know you guys do this…"

I socially engineered credit card companies to up the limit on the card. I wasn't really going to buy the sofa, but they didn't know, so I'd go and spend the £3,500 on something else. At 17 I got a credit card with five grand on it and a mortgage. I didn't know anyone else who had that at my age. But I was watching Tara and figuring it out, paying all the bills and building my credit rating in the process – and then they raised limits, and I saw they were throwing around cards with 10 or 15 grand on them, all with balance transfers as well!

What's a balance transfer? "Well, sir, if you take out this credit card, seeing how much money you owe on the others, we'll add to a nice new credit card for you and double the limit." Thanks, can I take one of them?! They were throwing it at us, and I knew I could take advantage of that.

We wanted to buy our own place – an 80s former council flat that Thatcher had sold off – and we went to Barclays to get the mortgage, but we didn't get it because I was too young. So, we went to Abbey National and paid a hefty deposit on it. I had some money in the bank – about £12,000 – and I only ever kept the cash at my nan's. I never took it when I moved, because I knew I wasn't going to be with Tara forever. Tara's dad was a caretaker, but he was also around some naughty people. I saw him get black sacks of cash, and watched how he hid it.

I'd always stored my cash under the bed at my nan's. I had a single cabin bed, raised off the floor with a desk underneath with wardrobes either side and a pelmet going round the outside of the frame. So, I asked my grandad, "Do you reckon you could put some hinges on that?"

He did, and when you pulled it down, there was a compartment all around the bed where I kept banknotes.

The Old Bill never found it when they searched me for the bike ringing equipment. Loads of people in my area knew I was dodgy, but none of them would have known the level I was already on. They used to call me Nasty Nick, after the EastEnders villain, Nick Cotton, and I hated it – he was a shitbag that stole from his mum. I would never steal from my nan or my mum.

I did have a temper. One night at two in the morning, I pulled up outside my nan's house in my Mercedes. I went in, and my nan was sitting up in her chair. She got up and walked away, holding her face. My sister Kate was sitting there crying, and she said, "Mark hit Nan."

Mark was Kate's boyfriend. I said, "He done what?!"

I went to the kitchen, got the carving knife out of the drawer, stuck it in my trousers, and pulled up outside his house. There was no answer, so I booted the door in and pulled the knife out. "Where is he?"

"We don't know…" his parents stammered.

"You're not leaving until he shows his face."

He came downstairs, and I wanted to plunge him. *You touched my nan.* I was so protective of her, and I was furious at him. I don't know what happened, but something came over me and stopped me.

I was capable of mindless violence. Once I hit a geezer around the head with a hammer in Southend because he laughed at me. Del and I were in my Renault 5 GT Turbo, and I thought I was Johnny Big Potatoes, revving the engine like a racing driver. But it had too much power for me, and the thing bolted to the left and I clipped the kerb. It broke the alloy wheel on the car.

These three geezers walked round, laughing at me. I got out of the car, fuming. "Fucking laughing, yeah?" I screamed. "Fucking laughing?" I went to the boot and got out the hammer. *They're taking the piss out of me* – over something trivial, but it didn't matter. I felt disrespected and in my world, you could not show weakness. At that age, everyone I knew and trusted used violence when they were disrespected. I pulled the hammer out. "You laughing now?" They cowered. "No, mate! No!" So I swung the hammer. I got in the car and drove off down the road. As we got down by the casino, I changed the tyre. He didn't die, but he wouldn't laugh at anyone who punctured their tyre ever again.

Violence had become totally normal to me, I was in my own bubble. I had spent my whole life witnessing arguments over things that really didn't matter, so if someone disrespected me, there was always going to be retribution.

The whole of the criminal underworld is like that. People get killed because of disrespect. If you let someone get away with disrespecting you and you don't deal with it, others will see you as weak. It's worse today, with social media. Disrespect online can get out of hand; and gangsters are online too nowadays.

Tara was an escape, though, and would take me away from my life for a while. I went abroad for the first time with her, to Tenerife. I had a week in the sun and loved it, partying every night in Las Americas, eating at all the nice restaurants that run along the coastline behind the main strip, all on my credit cards: "Buy Now, Pay Later". It was as close to a normal life as I had come, but I was starting to realise that I was not normal.

CHAPTER TWELVE

Crime Tips from the Old Bill

One day I was sitting at my kitchen table in my new flat, which Tara and I had just bought in Wimbledon. I was 18, and it was a Saturday afternoon. I was watching the football, trying to live a straight life, and wondering what my next move was going to be, when I heard a knock on the door.

"Police! Open up!"

I kept the door on the latch as I opened it to the two Old Bill in uniforms. *What's this all about? Am I in trouble?* "We're afraid to inform you, sir, that you have been the victim of a crime. Can we come in and talk to you?"

Victim of a crime?! This must be some sort of stitch-up, surely. But from the way they spoke, I was ninety-nine per cent sure they weren't lying so they could nab me. Still, I didn't want them in my flat, so I came to stand outside the door. "What do you mean, a victim of a crime? I'm not aware of any."

Not long before, I'd rented a car. We were having Tara's Mini roof chopped off and turned into a convertible, so we needed a car. It was a new shape Orion in navy blue, with all the extras. The people in the car hire office were dodgy, so they'd cloned my card and used it.

That explained the row I'd just had with Tara: my credit card bill had just come through, and she had taken a look at it to see what I was up to. She accused me of staying at a hotel in Blackheath with other girls! Ironically, I had come back to Greenwich at the same time as they used my card. Another thing had come up on the credit card bill: I'd spent £400 on chat lines. At the time, I assumed I'd cloned my own card by accident and given it to Salty or one of the boys to use before I left with Tara.

I came over with the Old Bill as if I was a concerned citizen, like that inquisitive kid at the bank, asking how fraudsters operated, and what the Old Bill was doing to catch them.

"Why don't we go down to the station and we can show you?"

Sounds good to me!

They took me down to the station, and a copper who was working out of the fraud squad told me everything. He said they'd been watching this car rental company for ages. And it was really clever, what they'd been up to. They understood the authorisation codes and the processes, what happened when a card got flagged up.

"If the card company thinks something dodgy is going one with your card," they explained, "they send a message to the PDQ terminal, asking you to call the authorisation centre to approve payment. The authorisation centre then asks you to answer a couple of security questions. They'll ask for Code 10 information, which includes your name, date of birth, and where you were born."

Generally, going to authorisation meant it was game over for that card. As soon as that happened you said, "Hold on, call me back in a minute," put the phone down, and scarpered. That card would then have a red flag against it, so it would have to be discarded.

But the Old Bill told me more: if you have two cards from the same batch and card 1 gets used at point A, then at point B, then card 2 also gets used at point A, then point B, you've got a problem. "At that point, the company will lock everything down and send all the cards to authorisation."

This meant that I could have thousands of card numbers from the same batch that would suddenly become worthless if just one red flag appeared. It had been happening a lot before I left Greenwich; that's why I'd needed so many grabbers and so many new numbers.

But what they told me next was amazing. "This dodgy car company has figured out that the ticket machines at train stations aren't connected to a phone line. It's all automated, so cards are automatically authorised and reactivated." Here I was, a criminal, sitting in a police station, getting crime tips from the police.

After a few rows and arguments, mostly over my spending on the credit cards, Tara and I decided we were going to have a break. I moved back to my nan's. She hadn't touched anything in my room: I guess she had known it wouldn't last. I was 19 and my wardrobe was something Kanye West would be proud of. I had a few quid parked up and Nan was happy to have me back at home. I was still playing street hockey, but now I played for the Brixton Yo-Yos. Pete, our old manager from the SE Warriors, was going to Ibiza.

I got some guys together from the team and said we should all go to Ibiza, take our kit and play some hockey in the day, before partying at night. We had one game of hockey the whole time we were there. We got so drunk and partied so hard that we ended up in different girls' apartments every night. It was a real boys' holiday: sex, drugs, and in our case, hip hop and R&B.

Someone at our apartment block had bought some tickets for Es Paradis, one of the super clubs, the one that looks like a pyramid. They cost £15, and were printed on normal paper, all in one colour. I asked the girl if I could look at one, and she let me have it. Del and I then slipped over to the photocopier, just behind the desk in the hotel's reception. I copied the same one on to one piece of paper until I had four to a sheet, then copied that sheet 20 times.

We cut all the tickets out, and ended up with 80 tickets to sell, so we went up and down the hotels, along all the beach at San Antonio Bay, and all around the West End. We made about 700 quid, which would tide us over until Del got paid two days later. After the week spent partying with all the Yo-Yo boys, I came back to my nan's and slept for two days straight.

So now I was back at my nan's. I was just doing little bits and pieces, working at LA Clothing in Chiswick, still trying to be normal, but the urge to steal was creeping back in. Crime has a funny way of doing that, like a drug: just that one slip, that taste of a little extra or something for free, and it grabs you and draws you straight back in. I could feel it coming again.

CHAPTER THIRTEEN

Star Seller

Throughout my criminal career, I often worked in shops. Not only was it a good front, but it also taught me the weak points I would be able to exploit for my own and my mates' benefit.

But once I knew how the trade worked, my entrepreneurial personality took over, and pretty soon I had five market stalls. From working in shops I learned that, if a brand like Levi's ordered a million shirts, the manufacturer made more. The surplus is known as "carbage", or cabbage. Once I found a wholesaler, I could buy shirts for £3 and sell them for £25. I bought all the equipment, the metal and awnings and racks, and I would start at 5 am, putting up stalls and setting up workers. At lunchtime I would go back to the shop in Willesden where I was working. On my way home, I'd pack away the stalls, put them in the van, and drive it home. I had the same routine every day. I wanted to succeed.

But my criminal urges had taken over again. I was young and single, and my ambition was ever increasing.

To understand more about consumer credit, I got a job in Currys, because they offered extensive credit agreements for electrical goods. I was a great at talking people into anything: sales was my name, and I was definitely sales by nature, no matter which side of the counter I was on. I became one of the star sellers, racking up £1 million a year in sales, but I was more interested in understanding the finance agreements.

When a customer came into Currys wanting to buy now and pay later, I would have to talk to the relevant finance company. I would say to them, "I think this one looks a bit dodgy to me, I want to see what they know." These new credit agreements were a bit like the scheme at Radio Rentals, where Monty had fitted them up with moody utility bills. The people who worked in there didn't have a clue what to look for when taking on new customers. This was the same. The finance company was reliant on the staff in Currys.

The finance company was telling me freely that when you got a dodgy one, somebody trying it on, or somebody who was lying about something, they didn't *really* know what to do. They didn't know how to check the identity documents they'd brought to show me in the store. I'd call the company, and they'd do a credit check on the customer. "Yes, that's all gone through, Mr Jones has good credit and had been accepted. Can you post the paperwork with the signatures? Thanks." There was no fax or email, or anything at all to confirm that the customer was who they said they were. They were just taking my word for it. They hadn't given me any training in how to tell if a driving licence or a utility bill was genuine, and if Mr Jones was who he claimed to be.

To get credit to spend in store, you needed something with your signature on. It was the same process as a store card: it was all about the information the finance company received. The shop used a finance company to get paid for the goods that you will receive, and the finance company in turn credit checked you to make sure you were worthy of finance. They did this by checking your credit score, and based on your financial history they then approved or declined you.

I learned about the companies that did finance for the different high-street chains: Lombard Finance, GE Capital, Lloyds and Clydesdale, which I learned was owned by Barclays Bank. I never personally stole anything from Currys – don't shit on your own doorstep. I did hit them one time, though, for 20 grand's worth all in one go, all on credit, using fake documents.

Not long before my 20th birthday I met Tanya, a barmaid who worked in the polo bar in Bexleyheath. She was short and very good looking. I had seen her loads of times when we went drinking in there on a Sunday night. It would be packed with girls from all over, all wearing the latest clobber and flashy bags. Then one night I went to a club called Zens in Dartford.

I was standing on the stairs trying to look cool when this pretty girl came up to me and said, "My friend really likes you."

"Oh yeah," I said, trying to sound casual, "where is she, then?"

"Over there."

She waved Tanya over, and we stood talking for a while before she gave me a goodnight kiss and her number. I gave Tanya a call the following Wednesday and we went out for a drink. She was quite shy, but we had a laugh and I really liked her.

CHAPTER FOURTEEN

Greenwich Again

My first son, Josh, was born on 22 September 1996. We had both passed out on the air and gas. Tanya woke me up, saying it was time. The baby was coming. Three or four hours later he popped his head out. That was the first life I brought into the world. It was an absolutely amazing, magical feeling.

I was doing great, I thought. I did what I had to do criminally, but now I was through the other side. I was 21, with a family to look after. In my mind, all I needed was Tanya and Josh. I sat with Josh in my arms for hours after he was born, just looking at his little face.

Our first year together was amazing. I really felt like I was starting to become normal. We had parties at our house, as well as going on holidays as a family together. I was a bit of a bubblehead, and I think that must have annoyed Tanya, although I didn't realise it at first.

I always had something else going on. Where we lived in Bexleyheath, I would park my car outside and get loads of parking tickets, and then have massive arguments with the parking wardens. They used to hide behind my front wall and wait, and at 9.05 am they would be all over it.

Tanya didn't like my argumentative side, but I couldn't change it. The combination of that and my criminal activities was never going to work for her. I never wanted to leave my child, especially as that was what had happened to me – but there was little love left in the relationship, and it wasn't working any more. So I left. But just before we split up, we tried to make it work one last time. We had been arguing, and I knew that wasn't good around our little boy.

I decided to take us all to America. Disneyland. Me, my nan, Tanya, Josh, my mum and John, and my little sister Kate. We rented a villa in Florida. My nan paid for it with money from my jobs. None of the others knew. I would always slip my nan loads of money, and I'd always buy her nice antiques, including a wine rack. By then, I think my nan had snagged where I was getting it from.

As I got older, my nan liked that I was a bad boy. Still, it was clear from our time in America that there was no future for me and Tanya. It was something I never wanted for any of my kids. I was going to stay around and support my kid as much as I could. My relationship with Tanya might have been over, but she never caused any issues with me seeing Josh. I did all the dad things with him: swimming, football, boxing. Like all working fathers, I could have been there a little more for him, but in general, he had pretty much the same upbringing as my others. Tanya has always been a great mother to Josh, and for that I'll always be grateful.

CHAPTER FIFTEEN

Phone Shop

I got to meet my brother, Alex, for the first time. He wanted to meet me, so I gave him Nan's address, and he borrowed a car and drove to London. When he arrived, I was upstairs in my room. He parked up and knocked at the door. My nan answered.

My brother is a monster. He is huge. I call him "Chewy". He had his hair in plaits, a bit like Pinhead in *Hellraiser*.

"Is Tony in, please?" he asked in his poshest voice.

My nan looked him up and down and shouted, "Tony, there is a pineapple at the door for you. Alex said he had never felt so little in his life. She made him change his hair, though.

I needed to start earning some proper cash. Back at Nan's, I considered my next move. My mate Barry had a phone shop, and he wanted to open another one in Greenwich and bring me in. The plan was that he would have the lease, and we'd work something out, splitting the proceeds of a shop he had wisely rented in a different name. He found a mule whose name he could rent in. That taught me that a mule could be used in any situation.

In the mid-90s, mobile phones became consumer goods, and shops began selling them on the high street for the first time. A lot of these companies were vulnerable on the mass market. Barry had worked for Carphone Warehouse, so he knew how to get the suppliers set up and how their contracts worked, and I knew how to rinse them. It was called "Phones for Who", and we looked the part in spiffy suits. You always need a bit of swagger with a con.

People came in, real customers, to get the new Orange or Mercury one-2-one phone contracts. Mercury (now T-Mobile) gave me £300 every time I connected a handset. If a customer wanted a Nokia banana phone, the curved one that slides out, they'd have to stump up £500. But you only needed 20 points to pass the credit check. And if you paid by direct debit, that gave you 18 points straight away. An address and a date of birth gave you two more points. No matter who came in, I'd say, "Don't worry, bruv, I'll get you a phone." I called the phone network and said, "I've got a customer who wants to pay by direct debit. Here are their address and date of birth."

"Hold on," I'd say. "The customer's changed their mind. They don't want to pay by direct debit anymore." But now it was too late, and they'd already passed the credit check. Then I'd say, "Can the customer take another handset out?" So now I was taking two handsets out on the same profile.

Because you got the money for the connection, Orange gave you £300 per phone. Plus, I got an extra handset that I could sell on. Each contract to us was worth a grand.

They paid the commission monthly, so you could whack it for a month and get a load of commissions. They had claw-backs, but it would take months. Claw-backs are where the network takes back the money they have given you for connecting the handset. We lasted for three months. Folded and legged it. But that was time enough to teach me a whole lot more about fraud. More lessons that money just couldn't buy, and more information banked.

About a month before we closed the shop, my dad had come out of the printing business. Not paying his tax fucked him up. You can't mess with the tax man. Not long before he had been driving around in a Porsche, but now he had to go cabbing. He wormed himself in with the owner of Star Cars, a cab office in Bermondsey. The phone shop had given me money to buy a car, and while I was still working there, Dad said, "Why don't you come and do a bit of cabbing?" Why not? I learned the roads, and met some interesting criminals.

One of the drivers in the cab office, called Alan, claimed I owed him money. Alan didn't know where the shop was so asked my dad, who told him where it is.

I was in the phone shop dealing with customers. The next thing, this guy Alan – ferret, we called him – came in the phone shop looking around. Up until this point he had always been friendly with me. I was like a big docile bear: play with me and I'm fine, but touch me and we have a problem.

I glared at him. "Why are you in my shop?"

Alan said, "I'm going to burn your car out."

I said, "Oh yeah, come on!" Was this guy mad? He was out of shape, and I was in my prime, plus he wasn't like me – he didn't have the pent-up anger, the rage inside that would destroy him in seconds. He didn't stand a chance.

"Show me where your car is." *This guy!* I'm thinking.

I came out of the shop, and as I was bending down to lock the door, he punched me on top of the head.

I turned. "Oh, you silly cunt. I'm going to smash you up. You started it." I booted him in the head, perfectly placed like Bruce Lee would have done. As he wobbled, I caught him with a right hook. *Good night mate!*

There was claret all over the floor, his face was swollen. "No more," he said, "that's enough."

I called my dad and told him I smashed Alan up. My nan turned up to see me in the shop just after it had all happened. She went mental at me and took this Alan, the ferret. She was always trying to protect me – she always knew I had a temper. I was no gangster. I'd done violent things, and I had stolen a lot of money, but I was never a gangster. I had only ever wanted to be normal.

When the phone shop was done, I went back to the cab office. But then fate played its hand. I took a Moroccan geezer from a flat in Raymouth Road to Tower Bridge Road. He had a beard and spoke in guttural clicks. He was like my mate T: he had a proper shady way about him. Criminals can spot other criminals, it's like we all have similar traits. I knew what to look out for. Just having a chat, I built up a relationship over the next few weeks with this guy, who kept calling me up, asking me to drive him places. By the end of it, he said, "I've got this move: do you know any girls?"

Not long before, while driving the cab, going into a shop to get a packet of fags, I'd spotted a girl cleaning the place out. She was called Michelle, and she was probably the best thief I'd ever seen. I got to know her, and drove her about for free, a lot of the time because I enjoyed her company. I used to call her Boots, because she'd hit the high street pharmacists and clear them out of Gillette Mach 3 razor blades, which are the most stolen item in the world, along with coffee and legs of lamb, apparently!

No matter how many alarms they put on them, she would steal all of them. I used to go in and watch because it was amazing how skilful she was at dispensing of the alarms that they stuck onto the packets? She would rip them off the razorblades and build all the alarms into a ball, and just throw it on the top shelf.

Criminality is about margins. Michelle had a geezer on a market stall who bought everything off her, at a decent price. He even inspired me to try and rob lorries, because he'd said if I robbed a lorry full of them, he'd take them all off me. He ran stalls at Woolwich, Deptford, Western International and Dagenham. This market trader lived in a five-bedroom house with a swimming pool, but I wasn't surprised, given the amount I'd accumulated while owning market stalls. And Boots the crackhead didn't do too bad, either. On the way back from a bit of work, she'd be on the phone saying, "Give me 20 white and 30 brown." That's crack and heroin. Then she'd buy three bags of weed and give one to me just for driving her.

"I like the sound of her," this Moroccan said, as we were going through the Blackwell Tunnel. "Fancy robbing a bank?"

I was obviously intrigued, because Stevie Edwards, the husband of Val who worked for my nan, robbed Barclays Bank with a pram. He pretended he had a baby in there, and when they were inside, they pulled the shooters out. They got caught and he got 15 years. I don't think that was the first one he'd robbed.

South London was a breeding ground for high-level criminals. Lee Murray's crew pulled off the UK's biggest ever cash heists, a £53 million raid on the Securitas facility in Tonbridge, Kent. They took the foreman's family hostage and wrapped up the staff with sticky tape. You've got to be proper ruthless or desperate to do that. I wasn't interested in that kind of robbery. "How are we getting it out?" I asked the Moroccan.

He produced a passport belonging to some rich girl from the university. Here was the really devious part: this guy would rent a flat in a shared house, make friends with the people in there, then when they were out for the day, he'd come in, take all their documents, and then withdraw the money from their bank accounts. "This bitch has got real money in the bank," he said. "I need someone who looks like her to go into the bank."

This wouldn't involve wrapping anybody up or pulling a gun, so I said yes. "Let's do it with Boots."

On Sunday he gave me all the woman's documents, including her passport. Boots looked a bit like the woman who was on the passport, but not much. She had blotchy skin and slightly hollow cheeks that this rich girl didn't. Also, she was a brunette with brown eyes, not a blonde. On the Monday I changed the picture on the passport, a skill Algerian T had shown me years before.

"Whoa!" the Moroccan said when I gave it back to him. "Who's that?!"

"That's Boots. Don't worry about how I did it, that's my job."

Boots got herself tarted up, and we drove her to a branch of Barclays in Wandsworth with the passport and birth certificate, having learned a few of her biographical details. The maximum you could withdraw in cash back then was whatever they had in their reserves. Whereas now, for anything over £3,000 they would be all over you.

We were sitting around the corner, waiting, waiting. She had been in there 10 or 15 minutes. "Don't worry," I told the Moroccan, who had started getting nervous, tapping his knee against the steering wheel.

"Are you sure?"

"Sure."

Now I was the one reassuring him, even though I knew you could never be a hundred per cent certain. Boots was good, she was experienced, cool under pressure, but you never know. There's always the possibility another person can let you down.

"There might be a queue," I said. "There's no reason for them to ask any questions."

"If you say so."

This Moroccan might not have been as seasoned as he made out. I was getting the impression that he'd never actually done this before. "They're not going to check, are they?" he said.

"Those documents are mustard, I'm telling you. That stuff she got is *real*. It's foolproof. Calm down, for fuck's sake."

Admittedly, there was a minuscule chance that one of the bank tellers had served the rich victim before and remembered what she looked like. But she lived in Mile End, and we had chosen a bank the other side of the city for that reason.

20 minutes later, when Boots came out with £15,000 in her handbag, I treated myself to more than just a Star Burger. I made the Moroccan take us all for a kebab and a shisha. Boots probably piped half of it, but I didn't care, because the next day she did the same again, and ordered £25,000 to be picked up on the Wednesday. Only then did it trigger a security alert –manual or computer, it wasn't important. All it meant was that they asked

her a few security questions. Back then it would be the place you were born and your mother's maiden name, and she knew all the answers, because we had all the information.

I came back home that week and stacked the money up on the side in my kitchen. The last time I'd seen Salty, I'd told him, "We're done, man, let's move on. I'll sell my equipment if you know anyone who wants to buy it."

But meeting with the Moroccan and doing the bank job with Boots triggered my criminal instincts again. So, I called an old friend, "Alright," I said to Salty on the phone, "fancy meeting up?"

"Of course, bruv", he said.

We met up in the cafe first thing in the morning. Salty was skinny as a rake. Egg, bacon, fried slice, tomatoes, beans, he ordered the full works. All washed down with a nice cup of tea. Our banter was like no other: we could talk in code and take the piss out of others by saying a one-liner that only we knew the meaning of.

If someone was telling a story and we thought they were lying, Salty would say, "Knock 6 foot off the fish." If I thought whoever was telling us the story was true, I would say, "Blow the candle out bruv!" He and I would know exactly what it meant, but no one else would.

On our own we were great, but as a team we were amazing. He told me that he had been whacking Debenhams. "They're good to go," he said, "you get a grand a pop."

"A grand, is that it?" I said.

"Bruv, it's fucking easy money and you can do five applications on five floors. All the department store are doing it." We decided that we were going to do this properly, a proper operation, me and him hitting the stores all over the gaff. Buy Now, Pay Never was back!

CHAPTER SIXTEEN

Buy Now, Pay Never

In Alders, they had leaflets for finance lying around everywhere. There were five levels in these huge department stores, selling everything from perfume to clothes to watches and televisions. Anyone could open up a finance agreement – Buy Now, Pay Later, just like back in Topman a few years before. Fill a form out in the car, go in, pick someone that looks like they are more interested in their nails, or selling you some perfume. Normally the people working on those counters didn't have a clue what to look for when it came to a false document like a driving licence.

So, I took a load of these forms, went outside, and filled them out in different names from the electoral register. Each profile was approved, with thousands of pounds worth of credit to spend in store that day. And to me, that was as good as printing money. I had buyers lined up all over the place who'd give me a percentage of the retail price of anything, from sofas and TVs to phones, watches and kitchens. My mobile phone was ringing constantly, with people from all over the UK wanting the latest goods at half price.

This was working. I was starting to get consistency as a criminal again.

I hooked up with the 419 guys – 419 being the number in the Nigerian criminal code for fraud. To commit multiple frauds, you need someone that can supply you with good, fake documents consistently, and this Nigerian bloke I knew could make them. His spelling left a bit to be desired, like most fraudsters, but he would be able to give us 10 driving licences a day – more than enough for me and Salty to be getting on with.

They always had their own crazy scams going on. One time they propagated an amazingly lucrative "black money" or "wash wash" scam.

Basically, they would lure people into hotel rooms and show them a suitcase full of money that had been dyed black, supposedly by Saddam Hussein or some other corrupt politician, and they needed a few thousand quid to acquire the solution to wash it clean. It was absolute social engineering at its finest, all taking place in front of your eyes like a magic show.

The first time I saw it, the cheeky cunts tried it on me, and I laughed at it. I could tell it was clearly just a confidence trick, because I used them all the time myself. "Alright," they said, "why don't you come in with us? You're like a Nigerian, you're a natural fraudster." Because I was white, so I added perceived legitimacy to the operation. One of my mates found a target: someone from the underworld who wouldn't be able to go to the Old Bill.

We brought him to a Knightsbridge hotel and introduced him to the Nigerians, and they pitched it to him. My role was kind of a hype man. When the mark saw the money, I jangled my Rolex watch at him, showing him my D&G labels, telling him, "I love these guys, look how rich they made me." As if to prove it was real, they gave the guy a grand of real money to spend, and we went out and spent it with him in a club. "You see, this ain't a scam, this is for real, bruv!"

So the guy went to the bank and transferred £70,000 to these Nigerian fellows to buy the solution to wash the money clean – and obviously, he never heard from us again.

Another time, they needed what they call a striker: someone who scores the goals. That was me – though I see myself more like Eric Cantona, a playmaker that can score goals.

The Nigerian said to me, "I have a move if you think you can do it."

"Oh yeah, what's that then?"

"I had a dodgy accountant who was ciphering of money into a separate account. There are over a million pounds in there. I want you to go into the bank and pull out half a million."

"Fucking hell," I said. "Half a mill, how the fuck can I get that out over the counter?"

"Don't worry, my friend," he replied, "I've got that covered."

And true to his word, he had it covered. The setup was great. The guy whose money we were stealing had been stealing it anyway, thinking that his dodgy Nigerian accountant had him covered. Just when you think they are doing this, they are doing that. The guy wanted to pay the accountant shit money for helping the guy siphon off all that cash. The accountant decided that he was going to take all the money and if I could pull it off, I would be handsomely rewarded.

It was a Monday morning. I met the Nigerian in the cafe, same as always.

"You look very smart," he said.

"Thanks, don't scrub up too bad, do I?"

He handed me over the paperwork and passport that he had made with my picture on it. He hadn't just done a picture change as I had with the Moroccan: he had made a whole new passport, all in the person's name that I was pretending to be. He told me that the accountant had ordered the money – they would, of course, want to do loads of checks, but they could just call the accountant and he would confirm everything.

I went in, straight up to the counter. I told the cashier I was there to collect some cash; it'd been ordered by my accountant. She asked me to take a seat.

Then another guy came over. "Hello, sir. Obviously, this is a lot of money that you are withdrawing – it will take a while, so would you like a cup of tea?"

"Thanks, two sugars, please."

I sat there for an hour. Still nothing. So I went outside and smoked a cigarette.

The Nigerian called me. "Everything ok?"

"Yeah, it's all good," I told him.

103

Another hour. Still nothing. The girls at the counter seemed like they were all looking at me – probably just my paranoia. I'd been in there two hours. *Calm down*, I told myself. I went outside for another fag and called the Nigerian. They had called the accountant, and he had confirmed everything was ok.

I went back in. "Mr Smith, come with me, sir," said the man. He took me to a little room inside the bank. The cash was waiting for me in the room – that made my arsehole feel a lot better. "Please count it," he said.

"It's ok, I trust you," I told him. I opened the Nike holdall I had with me and put all the cash in, then left the bank.

As I left the Nigerian was pulling up. I jumped in the back of the car and away we went. The feeling you get from being drunk on money is amazing. It's like for a little while you are a king. We were excited, jumping up and down. "Tonight, we party," he said in his Nigerian accent. That was the biggest amount of cash I had pulled out in one go. It satisfied my selfishness for a while, but of course, it was only covering up my insecurities.

I used his moody driving licences as identification for my jobs. What neither of us knew at the time was that a man and woman have different driving licence numbers. One day, when I was trying to open up a finance agreement in a store, it came on top: the credit company said there was something wrong with the identification documents. The staff on the shop floor couldn't tell, but when they rang it through to the finance company, they insisted the numbers were wrong. As they were having this conversation on the phone, I was listening in.

"So if a woman is born in a zero month, on her driving licence it will be indicated with a 5? That doesn't happen with men?" The finance companies worked out that if the number was wrong on the date of birth, the DL must be fake. Say I was born in month 01. If I was a woman, instead of saying 01, it would say 51. This idiot I was working with hadn't realised the difference.

"No worries," I said to the shop floor assistant. "I'll have to call the DVLA and get them to fix it."

"Yeah, sorry about that, darling, come back when you've got it sorted and we'll make sure you get that bracelet for your nan."

Then I rang the Nigerian and told him, "Change the fucking number."

"What do you mean?" he said.

"I mean the driving license number is wrong. You've been putting woman's fucking number on them, and you nearly just got me nicked," I growled at him.

"Ok, I'll sort it out," he told me.

The next day he did as I'd said. I went into another branch, and bang, it went through. Because this guy was not on the front line committing fraud himself, he didn't understand that the systems and processes of these finance companies were changing. They were starting to get much smarter – or the tech behind them was. And the Nigerian's tech skills were becoming outdated.

I wanted to make our own documents. We were upscaling. The Nigerian had given me an idea. He didn't go into the bank, but he still took most of the cash because it was his move. Salty and I would go in, but we were going to be making our own materials. We could build a team with better paperwork than the ones we could buy from the Nigerians, without all the stupid mistakes and shit. After all, we had done it before with the cloned cards.

The perfect credit profile is a 750-point credit score. That's the sweet spot for any bank, building society, or finance company. It means you have got a history of credit and borrowing, and you can be trusted to make the repayments. Things had moved on a bit since I first went to the library all those years ago, to steal Mr Patel's identity. The technology was starting to make decisions instead of humans. It was taking over everywhere. You could even get the electoral roll on a little disc called an "info disc". I had the pro edition. It had everything on it: names, addresses, dates of birth.

This was still a long time before GDPR. Data protection regulations existed, but they were struggling to keep up with the amount of data we were starting to compile. To keep up, the government would have to up their game with many new rules and regulations to help protect people's data. Data was the new cash.

I had a laptop, so I no longer needed to go to the library. I could just use the pro edition CD – it held every bit of info I needed, from names and addresses to company information. I could type "Tony Sales, England," and it would show me all the people called Tony Sales in England. I only needed to print a debit card with "MR T SALES" on it to imitate several people. I'd need a printed British Gas bill with "Tony Sales" on it, because one form of ID had to show the full name, but I could reuse the credit card with multiple identities: Tom, Terry or Tony Sales. I also had an A. White, A. Brown, and all the common names, like Smith and Jones. There were thousands of W. Smiths and P. Joneses all over the country, and that enabled me to choose somebody who was close to my age and lived in a nice area. I could even find information about company directors; that was really valuable, because they were likely to be wealthier than the average person and have a high credit score.

So, Salty and I decide we were coming back, and we were going to smash the granny out of it. Anyone who did credit agreements. Buy Now, Pay Never!

We decided to hit B&Q, House of Fraser, Homebase, and the like. Just searching for "store card" gave us a vast array of options. Who did finance? Comet, Currys, Argos, Alders, Ernest Jones, Goldsmiths Jewellers, Watches of Switzerland, Bentall Centre Kingston. The credit boom was in full swing, and we understood it like no other. All clothes shops now did finance – that's where I'd started.

All major retailers did it by then. That's how finance works: the more debt people have, the richer the finance companies become. And all of us are socially engineered to want the next iPhone or the latest tablet. I've seen five-year-old kids with a better phone than me, all paid for on the never-never.

From working in Currys and testing this system myself, I knew that the only risk was convincing an untrained salesman that your documents were real. Some people we were imitating would get turned down because they had a low credit score, but so what? We would just walk out and go somewhere else with a different profile. If our IDs were as good as they should be, there was no risk.

After all, how is somebody supposed to tell you that you're not who you say you are? That your name is something different, that your address is somewhere else when you've got all the paperwork to prove it? If I claimed my name was David Smith, and I had a driving licence in that name, a utility bill proving my address in Hemel Hempstead, as on the electoral roll, and a credit card with my name on it, how could anyone dispute that? Most of the time, minimum-wage clerks aren't interested in disproving it anyway. People only know what you tell them.

The best frauds were the ones where we let them sell it to us. When the salespeople were working on commission, they *wanted* to approve us! And what I'd learned from Currys was that retailers and finance companies made a huge killing not only from the interest on finance agreements, but from selling warranties. If a customer was looking to spend £10,000 and also wanted to take out a warranty that cost them absolutely nothing, there was even more incentive for them to let the customer have it. So wherever possible, we would always take out warranties, insurance, every type of add-on they had to offer – because it also made it look like we were responsible people who wanted the items for personal use.

And that was the brilliance of it. Unlike other thieves, who have to smash and grab and sometimes shoot their way in and out, we were *allowed* to take those TVs, sound systems, watches and cash out of the bank. They wanted us to have it. Why rob a jeweller or a bank with a gun when you can do it with a piece of paper? They even smiled and said thank you, holding the door open for us on the way out!

CHAPTER SEVENTEEN

The Counterfeiters

Most naughty people have had to lie to people in positions of authority since childhood, so changing identities for a few minutes is a piece of cake. You remember a name, date of birth, address, postcode, and star sign. You learn to fold up the utility bill in such a way that when you hand it over, you can still see everything that's on the pad. Just as in *The Usual Suspects* when Kevin Spacey reads his alibis off the wall, we'd do it for them live in store, turning their own greed against them, giving them the stories they wanted to hear so they could sell us their products.

As I started to understand credit companies, I realised there was a bit more to it: Goldsmiths and Hitachi's finance people wanted to confirm our work details. But that wasn't a problem. If I went for a watch in Goldsmiths that cost £20,000, it was certainly worth me spending £10 on a phone number that I could divert to my mobile.

"Hello, AK Builders, how can I help you?"

"Hello, this is Goldsmiths in Croydon. We're just

running a credit check and need to confirm a couple of work details. Can I confirm that David Smith is one of your site managers?"

"That's correct, do you need anything else?"

"Yes, we're obliged to check that his monthly earnings match what he has told us."

"Okay, I'll put you through to Accounts... *Hello, Accounts!*"

It was what the Nigerian had done when I took the half a million out in cash: we could easily confirm a few work details that we had made up in the first place.

If I was in the shop, Salty would do mine, and vice versa.

We had all the card-punching equipment from before. But we were moving onto driving licences, utility bills, bank statements – and we didn't have the equipment for that.

As well as a top-of-the-range *Mission: Impossible*-style laptop, I bought the best laser printer on the market to do utility bills. (A laser printer is best because it throws powder at the image – it's what big corporates use, and it works faster than average.) But I also needed templates. How could I get images of bills onto the computer so I could edit them? I scanned my own gas bill and printed it out. But I realised straight away that the colour had changed. There was a change of tone where the light had crept in. There were also crinkles from the imperfections of the paper, and gradients instead of block colours. It looked like an impression of a gas bill, rather than an actual gas bill.

This was going to be harder than we imagined. Especially since I had never really used a computer before. I had taken ICT classes at college, but I hadn't lasted long there. Long after I left school, I tried to get myself a better education. At 17, I enrolled at Erith College. I had to leave, though, as they kept asking about fees. I was 17 – without crime, where was I supposed to get the money? So I left and went back to crime full time.

All these computers were a new world for me. I was just messing about with the programmes that came with the laptop. When I opened one of them, I saw the "Cut" option. Then there was one that said, "Fill". *Oh, it's gone black. How do I change that to blue?* There was a dropper – *What does that do? Oh, I can take the colour from over there and fill this space with it.* So, through trial and error, I figured out how to blank the boxes and retype them with the names and addresses I wanted.

I had never heard of Photoshop or Coral Draw back then, and certainly didn't have any idea how to layer a document, but my mind was built for this stuff. I sat at that laptop for 24 hours straight making a British Gas bill. It looked pukka by the time I had finished. I was doing it in Microsoft Paint, and that was no easy thing to do.

To make the perforated edges, I went to a stationer and looked at their guillotines. The stuff I had learned working at my dad's printers made me think, *They must sell something that can help me cut this paper.* Then I saw it: a skip blade. It was like a little wheel razor blade that left whatever you rolled it over with a perforated edge.

When you get a bill, what is at the bottom? It says Giro Bank Credit. That's so you can go into the bank or post office and pay the bill. So, I made a stamp that said "Paid". I ran along the top of where it said Giro Bank Credit with the skip blade and pulled it off in a straight line. It looked perfect, with the perforated edge just like a real one.

We had the kit, so now it was time to build the team and upscale. We were about to change the landscape of fraud and financial crime forever.

Salty and I had decided we were going to be an organised criminal syndicate. We were going to need workers who would go out and graft for us. So, I started to recruit a street team. They would have to be habitual liars who were desperate for cash.

My cousin Jo's friends were all addicts: that would be a good place to start. I was now the money man. I'd pull up in a nice car and peel a few notes out my shirt pocket to give to him – they would see this and it would always pique their interest. They would ask me, "Got any jobs you need doing, Tony? Or am I going to have to go choring?" People with addiction problems were always in need of some graft: they had to feed the addiction coming from the trauma most of them had suffered as kids, just like me.

The thing is, you can't just take any smackhead or alcoholic and make them work. When someone wanted to come and graft for me, I had to make sure they had your wits about them and could hold it together in a tense situation. But I didn't want to be known as the mastermind behind any of this. I was constantly aware of what might happen if they got caught, and the links back to me. The police trying to set me up with Eve had shown me how far they would go to catch criminals who were easy targets. Most people who worked for me after that only ever heard my voice on the phone – a bit like Charlie and his angels. The only Charlie these workers cared about, though, was the type that gets washed up.

Salty and I put word out that we were looking for people, and give them a number to call. "I got a way of making money if you're up for it. Let's meet at Burger King, 10 am." I chose Burger King because they didn't have CCTV. I knew most of them, so I'd go into the toilets and stash the identity paperwork inside the toilet roll dispenser. Then I'd message them telling them where to get it. Sometimes other people took it, or maybe wiped their arse with it and flushed it down the toilet. But usually, I'd be watching them go in to collect it, then I'd tell them to memorise the details and go into the Orange phone shop, where they only asked customers for a card, name, address and date of birth.

The good ones would go in and get one or even two phones. Or they'd ring me and say, "They've offered me a laptop, shall I get that as well?" They were the ones I wanted. The ones who called me and sounded worried, saying "They're going out the back to check..." were clearly not up to it. One of the boys would always be in the shop watching them. Jim Bobby was good at that – observing without being noticed. Once they'd got their phone or their laptop, I let them keep it and told them to put the paperwork back. I'd be in contact tomorrow.

The next day they would get a call.

"We're going to go out for the day. TB is going to come and pick you up. He'll supply you with the paperwork. The name is A. Smith. Your mate is A. Jones. Here are Mr Smith and Mr Jones' documents with all the info. Make yourselves familiar!"

I'd give them a little bit of time, then I would tell them what to do.

"Brenet's in Essex will give you £5,000 in each store. We're going to hit four shops, so you'll get £20,000 in total to spend. I'll give you the brands of TV to get, and you'll put them in the van that's waiting in the car park."

CHAPTER EIGHTEEN

Meet the Team

"Sinner" was a scrawny little white guy, a Millwall football fan who was robbing doorstep collectors. I met him in my early twenties through family connections. His folks never gave a fuck about him, so I'd take him round to meet my family, and I became a kind of godfather figure for him. The kind of doorstep robberies he'd been doing, where he'd scare the living daylights out of people and bundle them into cars, weren't sophisticated at all. He paid the price for that by going to prison every three months from an early age.

When he was looking at a long stretch for aggravated robbery, I sat him down and asked, "Is this really what you want?" After that sentence, he came to work for me. We started out hitting phone shops, and he was a natural at it. Just put a whistle on, as he'd say, and he could be very charming. In fact, Sinner got us one of our most valuable bank insiders. A girl who worked in a local bank wanted him badly, so he took the opportunity. He called me up one day and said, "I'm humping a pig!" Criminals will always look to exploit an insider if they can – social engineering is devastating to any business. That gave us a safer way of passing cheques and doing money transfers. It also gave us access to valuable information about things like dormant bank accounts.

"A-Class" was a drinker and a bit of a fantasist, but if you know how to manage people, both of those things can be advantageous. A-Class had a great routine that nearly always worked: he'd tell shop assistants who might be sceptical about whether he could afford luxury goods that he was an international DJ who played to crowds of 20,000 people. In reality, he could barely change a cassette tape in the van, but it didn't matter. A-Class was a quality guy, but a bit of a liability when he got too pissed. We'd be in a nightclub having it big, and he'd come out prancing around in some dweeby glasses. "What you got them on for? Whose are they?" I'd ask. "Some geezer I just chinned in the toilets, I've left him slumped in the urinals. He was looking at my dick. We'd better get out of here."

"TB" was a big-time drug dealer who'd fallen on hard times. Over-fed, well-dressed, of Turkish or Armenian origin, he looked every bit the successful businessman. He was used to living the high life, so knew all about luxury goods. That is, until he got robbed by one of the scariest motherfuckers in London, a proper notorious gangland guy called DB. TB was a bit of a fantasist too. He would say a lot of things that were true, then spin bullshit around it.

"Favor" was a Turkish geezer who was always saying, "Do me a favour, do me a favour." We'd started hanging around in Brighton because there was a really bad heroin problem down there. It was a skill of ours to spot crime happening elsewhere. We would hang around, watch what was going on and talk with people, get to know them. Fava wasn't a junkie himself – he worked in a kebab shop and had no history of fraud – but he was selling coke. We recruited him because we knew he'd be subtle, and he could make way more for us than he could knocking out £50 wraps on the side.

"Salty" was a slick bastard who was ripped to fuck, with more charm than P Diddy, and probably more money. He was a master of social engineering. We used that to our advantage when choosing which sales assistants to target. Salty was the first one to talk a female bank teller into playing ball with us. Sex is the best social engineering tool ever, male or female. But Salty was also one of the most sensitive people I have ever met. Strong people usually are.

I was known as "Hotts" – not because I am hot, more of a hot-head.

There were 10 workers going out to begin with, a motley crew of people with different issues: drink, drugs, debts. Not all of them were exactly criminal geniuses, but we were, and we found a pattern that worked for us and them. Growler, for example, was a junkie. He had very sticky fingers. He could barely get finance on a phone, but he'd always want to go out. He drove me mad, always calling me up. I'd hear his deep gruff voice: "Tone, I need to graft, bruv". He was a nightmare at times. If he was having a bad day, he'd go and nick the shoes off a mannequin in a shop window, just to make himself look better. Really, he should have nicked a fat suit, because he was only about two stone. Then there were the likes of Boots, regulars who'd always be up for scoring big, as well as others who would dip in and out.

Lightning, Bob the Knob, Gary B, and the ugly sisters. Most of them had no idea who I or Salty were, or that I was orchestrating it all with Salty. Those who did know were under strict instructions: if they got caught, they must not say anything about me or Salty. Trust was gained and not just given. As far as they were concerned, I was just a middleman, another member of the team, or a driver.

The transport crew were vital for organisation and logistics. When you pick up a new TV, you don't want them all piled up in the back – that looks dodgy. Both Salty and I had worked in shops, so we understood what looked dodgy to others, and it worked well. We had a fleet of people carriers and vans to ferry the teams around and collect the goods.

Salty and I would test out the stores on our own, and then when we sent the crew in, we tended to hang back. But we had the most difficult and high-pressure role, organising the jobs – we earned our money.

"Lightning" wasn't very quick: I called him that because he drank White Lightning cider. He was a good-looking kid, I liked him, and I thought I'd take him out for the day. I knew he was a drinker, but didn't realise how bad it was until I went to pick him up at 8 am. He was lagging. I sent him home and told him if he wanted to work with me, he would have to be sober.

I told him that I would be back at 8 am again tomorrow to pick him up, and if he wanted to come out, he would have to be sober – no addiction on the job, no exceptions! The next day he was as sober as a judge, and we headed out down to Kent. I wanted to ease him in to this nice and smoothly, so I took him to Canterbury.

I sent him into a phone shop and it all came on top – he was caught. When that happens they will either just turn you down or call the police. That was where Salty and I came in.

The shop staff weren't police, so even if they suspected us, they couldn't do much in the moment apart from call the police. They didn't have the authority to take their phones off my workers, who would be on the phone to me, pretending I was their missus.

"Alright, sweetheart?"

We would use our own code and have conversations with the workers while they were detained to find out what was going on.

"What's happening, is it on top?" (Have you been caught?)

"Yeah, I'm going to be staying away tonight." (Yes, and the police are coming)

"Do you want me to pick you up?" (Can I intervene?)

"Yeah, please if you can."

At that point, we instigated the plan: as soon as Lightning put the phone down, Salty went into the shop.

Once he was inside, I rang the business and asked to speak to the manager while Salty listened in, monitoring their reactions.

"Hello, is that Phones4U in Canterbury?" I said. "It's Detective Sergeant Marks here. I believe you've just had to detain somebody? I'm going to send a detective in to pick him up now, is that okay? We need to keep moving really quickly, because this is a really organised gang. Thanks, we'll be there in five minutes."

I had a long, straight black leather jacket that looked like an Old Bill coat, and a smart pair of shoes. I was big and imposing, and I'd use body language and tone of voice to make it clear that I was in charge. We had a badge we had bought; it was out of date, but the ER part looked the nuts. And, of course, I had my mouth. Social engineering works in many ways. I went in, flashing the badge.

"Hello, Detective Marks sent me".

"Blimey, that was quick."

"Yes, I'm part of a special undercover team, we've been watching these guys for ages. What happened? … Yes, that's using a fraudulent implement with intent, well done for spotting it! Where is the toe-rag?" I asked.

"Out the back, officer."

"Do you have CCTV? Could I have the tapes, please? And all the documents he used? I'm going to have to bag them. Let me put the suspect in the van."

So I took all the evidence, chucked it in a bin liner, and then we were out of there. I didn't even have hand-cuffs.

Lightning had got caught because when you're having licences made in bulk, the names are sometimes wrong. You might have Mark spelt "Msrk", because of a sloppy typo. I always told the workers, "Make sure you check your ID before you use it," but Lightening obviously didn't look.

There are times when people get nicked and you can't save them. I wasn't going to bail everybody out. Captains and newbies I always would. And if they did get nicked, nobody knew anything about me. They'd met me, but they didn't know who I was. Because I was an undercover boss.

"I got picked up by this geezer, I don't know what his name is." That's what they'd say when they got picked up. Human nature meant that most people would say whatever might get them off taking responsibility – even if it meant giving me away. I knew that every person was a potential liability who could let me down – after all, most people in my life had let me down at some point.

Little Del Boy that I was, I'd been wheeling and dealing on the black market around London since I was a kid, so I knew the dodgy dealers in every area. I wanted a couple of guys that could buy in bulk. That would keep my business away from too many people – loose lips and all that! There was one guy who bought all my TVs. He'd been nicked since I'd been selling them to him, and he didn't grass me up, so I trusted him. Same with all the other gear like phones and watches – one guy who I trusted would buy them all off me.

One of the guys would call me up and say, "Hotts, I need 10 tellies, three Rolexes and seven kitchens." They'd want them from a very famous store, and they'd come to me because they knew I could do it. I had consistently delivered; my reliability had almost become a brand. To get that notoriety, you need all the cogs in the engine to function. That's why police take out crime groups piece by piece: in a well-oiled machine, it is hard to identify the linchpin that holds everything together. For me, being able to deliver was key. If my guy called me up to make an order and I didn't deliver, my ratings would go down. I always made sure whatever they ordered never took longer than 48 hours to deliver, no matter the amount.

On the rare occasions where the thing I stole didn't work, those warranties we took out in store weren't much use. But I would always try and replace it for them. That happened with one of Lee Murray's crew. A TV I got him malfunctioned, so I went out and tried to replace it. But they didn't have the model he wanted, so just like M&S, I gave him his money back. Not many criminals have a refund policy.

We kept close control of the teams without any of them knowing. The captains' and our phones would be ringing non-stop. Again, everything would be done in code.

"You alright, babe?" I'd say on the phone.

"It's all good babe, I'll be home for dinner," they would reply.

"Well done, love ya, get home safe."

I'd play them all off against one another. "You beat him this week." That kept them competitive. I would only ever pay them once a week, but I'd always end up giving them subs. The captains would call me up and say, "The ugly sister need some food for bruv." The captains always had the cash, but would just call to check. They knew not to give our money away.

Every Friday I'd pay everyone out their wages. I always gave a little prize to the best workers – usually a gram of coke, a crate of beers, or whatever their vice was. Sometimes we'd go to a club or even a whorehouse, and I'd treat the boys. Although the ugly sisters probably needed it more, it was all on me. I wasn't flashy about it, because show-offs get caught, and of course jealous eyes are dangerous.

I went to John Pinto's funeral, which was my first proper introduction to Dave Courtney. There were loads of his crew: all these gangsters who dressed like the mafia. The whole green at the top of my road was covered with flowers and wreaths. There were blokes with long black trench coats and bald heads everywhere. My mate Cyril said to me, "Look how hot all that is." That was a lesson I would have paid for, and I got it for free. Even today, I'm most comfortable in the shadows.

A few weeks later, four of the captains got nicked, all on different days. Crime always comes to an end at some point, and someone has to be punished. I came back home that week and stacked the money up on the side in my kitchen, and knew I needed a break from crime for a bit. So I went and bought a red Mercedes 190E

Cosworth, all lowered, alloys – it looked the absolute nuts, and I went back to the cab office for a while to let the heat cool off.

We went to Caesars in Streatham, with its big chandeliers and staircase leading down to a huge dance floor. They played all different types of music: pop, R&B, ragga, and a bit of house and garage. There was a good mix of people in there. It was one of the rare clubs we liked. No one in there was stuck up. Just loads of people enjoying themselves. I was doing my dad dancing, Salty was giving it the pistols, Del was doing his hair, and Danny Bleach was standing around trying to be cool.

We were standing there when these two girls come over to us. One had big green eyes, and they both looked like they were having a good night. "Give us a chip," one of them said to me, so I threw a couple of chips their way. As they got in the cab, the blonde one gave me a cute little smile. They left, and we headed home.

Two weeks later we went there again, this time for my 23rd birthday. As it was my birthday, there were around 30 of us in there that night. While I was standing talking to Salty, the same girl who had asked for a chip a couple of weeks before walked past with her friend. I stopped her and said, "Same again tonight, I'll buy ya some chips."

She laughed.

"What's your name?" I asked.

"Lynn," she replied.

We talked all night. I was making her laugh, all my mates were dancing, the atmosphere was great and we all had a really good night. Lynn and I danced the night away, we kissed, and at the end of the night she asked for my number. At this point, I had been working in the cab office doing the controls, so I gave her the cab office number. We kissed again and left.

It was a Wednesday night, around 7.30 pm. The radio was going in the cab office and the phones were ringing non-stop. "Tango four zero, you want the Foresters, corner of Gallywall Road. Three one, you want Lou Farrell's in the blue, going to Surrey Docks."

The phone rang and I answered it. "Hello, Star Cars."

"Hello, can I speak to Tony please?" I heard a cute voice on the end of the phone say.

"Yeah, it's me. Hello, I was hoping you would call!"

I sat chatting to Lynn for ages. We got on really well, and she was so level-headed. We arranged to go out for a drink the next day. I spent hours getting ready. Finally, I went to meet her, and we had another good night eating and drinking for hours, just enjoying each other's company. She was a good-looking girl who took care of herself and seemed to be doing ok in life too.

CHAPTER NINETEEN

Cocaine & the Nightclub Incident

I'd been seeing Lynn for around a year, and was keeping my nose out of trouble. She lived over in Worcester Park. She liked to party every now and then, but generally my life was way more mellow and controlled when I was with her, and I needed that. My nan really liked her.

"She's a good one," Nan said. "Don't fuck it up."

I had not been out with Salty for ages, until we arranged to meet up to go to a club in Southend called Adlib (now Chameleon). There was a DJ on who Salty wanted to see. I picked him up in my red Mercedes. In the glovebox there was a 2.2 gun that was supposed to have been reactivated. I had it in there just in case. I had bought it off someone who told me they fixed deactivated ones. I had sniff in the car, but I hadn't had any yet. Since I'd been with Lynn I'd been good: she didn't do it, so no need for me to either.

We got to the club. I had a JD and coke and Salty had a lemonade – he has never drunk a drop of alcohol in his life. There were loads of bods I knew in there, and I was bubbling. We danced, enjoying ourselves. I had had a few drinks, but I wasn't lagging. Someone had dropped a drink on the floor, and I bent down to pick it up. I stumbled as I got up, wobbling all over the place. The doorman rushed me, hands behind back, bouncing my head off the door, and I was out in the alleyway.

"What the fuck you doing?!"

"You're drunk."

"I came here to get drunk. I'm having a good time. I didn't do fuck all wrong," I told him.

"Don't get lairy."

"Let me go and get my mate, and we'll leave."

"What's your mate's name? We'll announce it over the tannoy. Stay there." Then he slapped me round the face.

That slap was one of those events which changes the course of your life. Stephen Parr, the local bully used to slap me round the face when I was a kid to humiliate me. All those feelings flooded back. I was humiliated again, but I wasn't a little kid any more. I was fuming. The red mist was descending on me fast.

From what I know now I can see that all the negative things in my life had built to that point. My mum, my dad, Beater Basher, all the bullying. I wasn't going to stand for it anymore. The rage inside me was like nothing I had felt before. The doorman had just awoken a sleeping bear. I'd been around violence my whole life, and this was my zone.

"Yeah?!" I said. "Watch this, I'm gonna show you."

I knew the gun was in the car, but the car was locked and Salty had the key because he was driving. I was booting the window to try to get in. I had gone into switch mode, and Salty knew that kind of madness. He laughed as he came out.

"You ain't gonna do nothin'! Come on let's go." Salty unlocked the car. We got in, and I racked a line up.

"Wait here, I need to calm down." I said to him.

I had a bottle of Cava in the car. I popped that open and swigged it. Chopped two lines up. Sniff, sniff. More coke than I'd ever had before. My teeth were going numb. I opened the glove box and got the gun out.

"What you doing?" Salty said. "Where you going?!"

"I'm not having it! Slapping me? Thinks he's a badarse?"

I approached the club, feeling the rage surging through my blood. As I got closer, the doorman spotted me.

"Oh, you're back." *Want another slap?*

I stepped back and unleashed the pistol. *You ain't fucking slapping me again.*

"What you gonna do with that, you fucking nutter? We'll call the cops."

"Think you're a big man yeah, watch this!"

I let the gun off. Bang, bang, bang.

Everyone screamed and dispersed. I was letting shots off into the crowd. The next thing I knew, I heard, "Put your hands behind your back!" There was armed police in the middle of Southend, surrounding the club. "Down on your knees!"

I woke up in the police station the next morning, dying for a piss. There was no toilet, so I went on the floor in the cell. "Oi!" I screamed. "What am I doing here?!"

I was starving and proper hungover.

"Bloody hell," the copper told me, "you've been a naughty boy."

"Really? Have I? What have I done?"

"Give me a minute, I'll get you a cup of tea and some breakfast."

A few minutes later he was back with a cardboard box containing my breakfast. Beans, sausage, and some sort of egg – all of it tasted like shit. The he took me into the interview room and showed me the video of me losing it with a gun. I was like John Wayne on cocaine, firing into a crowd. Everyone dispersed around me, and I was sitting there thinking, *I can't believe that's me.* In my head, I was wondering how many I'd killed.

"Lucky that was a blank firer," the cop said.

That was a huge relief. The guy I'd bought the gun from had ripped me off! It wasn't reactivated at all, but the previous night I didn't know that. I felt embarrassed at what I had done, but it was one of the best lessons I learned. It took that type of violence out of me, because I realised I was capable of it. I don't know what I was thinking.

I told my lawyer I'd got the gun to frighten foxes in my nan's garden. Still, they charged me with possession of an imitation firearm with intent to harm. So, I got a naughty charge, and I went guilty to it.

They bailed me that Sunday at 6 pm. I got my phone, rang my nan and asked if grandad could come and pick me up. I told her I had been nicked.

"I've got Lynn here, we're all petrified. The police have been here and confiscated bullets from the house."

Oh my god, what else have they taken?

Not a lot else, as it turned out. They hadn't found any of my card-strapping equipment or moody cards – or if they had, they didn't know what it was about.

It took over a year from my arrest to sentencing, so in the meantime, thinking I would probably lose my freedom, I went on holiday to Mexico. The court asked for security, which we paid into the court. They hold it just in case you run away, a bit like a bail bond that they have in the US.

I went to Mexico with nan, grandad, mum, good John, sister and Lynn. We got drunk for two weeks, partying every day. We hired speedboats and drove through the mangroves, to the most beautiful reefs. We went Scuba diving, miles out to sea. We went to an island on a pirate ship. Went to a fair where I saw people with two heads, and cows with five legs. We had a hired guide, Eric, who showed us things that you just don't see as a normal tourist. After jetskiing, we went to a well-known bar called Carlos n Charlie's – big neon sign out front – one of the few places where you could get label-brand drinks like Jack Daniel's. I spent about £2,500 in the bar, then went back to the hotel, El Pueblito, a beach resort place. We were there for the millennium New Year's Eve celebrations in 2000, and went out to party in silly hats.

At the time, El Chapo was going to war, and you had rival firms running the buses and taxis. The buses came like taxis – you didn't have to wait, and they'd take you wherever, because they were so competitive. It was like Miami with the malls, beachfront hotels and bars. It was a really beautiful place, all set along the Caribbean Sea.

Eric took us round. "£200 for two weeks," he said, "and I'll show you Cancun." He took us to Pepe's private zoo. It was a special place where they kept lions, tigers and jaguars. Many famous people came from America to visit Pepe's. You could even swim with a liger. Officially, Pepe's had been closed by the Mexican government, but he had got jaguars in cages, feeding them whole chickens. He says, "You want to see a panther?" I did. He brought a baby panther out, and I stroked and petted it.

It was my birthday while we were out there. My nan arranged us a trip on a pirate ship, with all these guys with swords. Everyone was dressed up in eye patches and big earrings. I got on the boat and this geezer kept saying, "Hey, you're Tony." They were pouring tequila down our throats, shouting, "To-Kill-Ya!"

We sailed to Isla Mujeres – "Women's Island" – and had a lobster banquet with tacos and Mexican rice. Everyone had to check underneath their seats. Whoever had the tag had to stand up. It was me. They dragged me up onstage, and it was my big moment, because I knew I had to go to jail when I got back home.

It was the best holiday I ever had. Lynn got pregnant out there. When we came home, I went to court, and got sentenced to two years – not bad for what I had done. These days I would get several times that. As long as I was good in jail, I would be out in time for Zack's birth.

CHAPTER TWENTY

Belmarsh Prison

They took me to Belmarsh Prison from Basildon Crown Court. Through reception, you go into what's called the Bubble, for the new arrivals. "Got a bit of burn, mate?" some bloke asked me as we sat there.

"No mate, sorry, it's my first time in," I told him.

"Don't worry, they'll give you an induction," he said.

"Induction, what's that?" I asked.

"They teach you all the rules, and all about prison life. You'll be going to Beirut."

"Why do they call it that?" I asked.

"Because just like in Beirut, you get fuck all there. No pillow or cover," he replied. They at least gave me a blanket.

I'd taken advice from old timers: a geezer called Gary Baldie who worked at the cab office, and a 90-year-old called Dick who'd lived through the war. He called me Lightning because I was so quick. Dick was a real wheeler and dealer in his day. He would tell me great war stories and how all the cabbing scams worked. "Go around the roundabout on the outside, you get an extra .2 miles on that trip. Makes it a fiver instead of £3.50."

He told me to use the sentence for good, but I told him about all the fraud I had done before I started at the cab office. He told me that as a young man, they'd wait for rich American women who were going to an abortion clinic in Harley Street. He said they would come out at Heathrow and you could just spot them, so they would go up and say, "Special service to Harley Street." He would drop them to the clinic, charging them a fortune. He said he could read their faces – he could tell what was on their mind. "Use your time to think about what you want, kid," he told me. "You only have one shot at life. Don't waste it!"

I'd been there about three months with a good job, working on the bins, sitting in my cell with the door open, when another prisoner walked in. "There's a new fellow here," he said, "called Darren Brennan." He was my mate from school, doing six years for robbery.

Opposite me on the wing was Razor Smith, who today is the editor of the prison newspaper Inside Times and has written books. He didn't socialise much, because he was into education and reading. He was about halfway through his sentence. Then there was Jamie Philips, whose dad I had worked for as a kid in Greenwich. Jamie's dad Jimmy was a notorious armed robber. He told me once that the Old Bill had threatened him: "Enough is enough, Jimmy, you do any more and we will iron you out."

Jamie was skipping in his cell. He had made a rope

out of the bed sheets. I thought, *What a good idea.* So, I went back to my cell and cut the laces out my trainers, twisted the bedsheet, and tied it all up. It was a really good rope. It never unravelled – it was super strong. I was skipping for weeks. I kept it under my bed.

One day, while I was out in the yard to empty the bins, I was sitting on the kerb having a fag, having a chat with the boys from New Cross, the Twins and Yankee. We were chatting away when the screws came over.

"Alright, guv?"

"Who's Sales?"

"That's me."

"Come with us."

It looked serious. I followed them onto the wing. I was worried it was about Lynn, because she was pregnant.

He said, "You'll see in a minute."

"Please can you tell me if it's my missus?"

"It's not."

I went into the wing office, and the PO was there with two pips. I didn't know what this was about. I hadn't been in any trouble: I was doing my education course in "enhanced thinking", I was a diligent worker, I hadn't chinned anybody or started any rackets, I hadn't touched any drugs – I was a model prisoner. I knew Lynn was pregnant, and I did not want to do anything to miss the birth of my child.

"You've got a rope," he said.

"Yes, I've been skipping." I laughed. I genuinely had been skipping, so I relaxed. I hadn't done anything wrong. So, nothing to worry about. Or so I thought.

The rules are different in jail though. Guilty until proven innocent.

"You brought me back for that?" I said.

"I don't think you realise the seriousness of this. You're in a Category A prison. *The most secure prison in the UK*. You work in the yards. You've got a rope. And you know people who are Double-A Category prisoners," he told me.

"Yeah, but I was skipping with it. Hasn't left my cell," I said.

They said they'd stop me working in the yards until I'd seen the governor. So, three days later I went to see the boss. There are two screws behind you at an adjudication, and they push you right up close to the table and jam you in with their feet on the back of the chair.

"See, guv'nor", I began – sticking to the story because it was true – "a PO popped the flap to my cell door during the night. He's seen me skipping. He's from house block 2. He can vouch for me." They said they'd checked it out, but couldn't corroborate it. As if he was going to stick up for me.

The Guv'nor said to me, "Get up and skip." And I did. Like Muhammad Ali, I skipped.

The Guv'nor says, "It's a month's loss of earnings, canteen, and remission."

"For what? Are you joking?"

Then he said, "Two weeks' G-O-A-D: Good Order And Discipline. That's total isolation, except for the Bible." The only human contact would be the screw bringing my meals in, who might be a listener if I was lucky. No radio, no tobacco, no exercise. Shower once a fortnight. I stuffed a bit of tobacco up my arsehole before they took me away. Funny what you will do for an addiction.

In the block cell, I was fuming. Two minutes later, DST: the designated search team crashed my cell, stripped me naked and told me to "Squat! Above the mirror." Luckily, I had just got the tobacco out and plugged it up in the Bible.

They took my clothes and put me in an E-Man suit. I was an escapee now, and I had A-Category security everywhere I go. When they were gone, I pulled a page of the Bible out and rolled a fag. I called the listener, because it was going to drive me mad, this isolation. I said to the listener, who was from my wing, "In my Bible there's a staple. I'm going to pull it out and pick my wrists. I want you to tell the screws, so they move me to healthcare." I picked the skin away and rubbed the two bloody wrists together. I was using social engineering, playing on all the emotions of human nature. I was sure it would work.

The screw popped the flap, looked in, and laughed. That wasn't what was supposed to happen.

All I could think was *Oh my god, he just laughed. I need to up the ante and pick them a bit more, make them bleed proper. Then they have to move me to healthcare, whether he believes me or not.*

It worked. In healthcare they gave me my stuff back. I was given a radio and a thorough psychiatric examination. I fluffed my way through it, keeping me in healthcare for the whole of that two-week adjudication. I had a single cell, and they even delivered me my canteen.

When I came back to the wing, all my mates were banging and cheering. It was an amazing atmosphere. When there was football on in there, or somebody chins a screw, the place would erupt like nowhere else!

I spoke to Razor. He put his arm round me and said, "Bloody hell, you been through it, boy. Come and look at this."

He showed me a photo of him standing on a bank's counter with a shotgun. In jail, I was beginning to meet bigger guys: they brought a casino cheat in called Frankie di Fasser from Malta who was living in Deptford at the time. He was a really funny guy who got six months for applying for a passport in somebody else's name so he could get into casinos, as he was blacklisted by them all.

He taught me a card game called Kaluki, a game played mostly in jails. He showed me how to look for cards that were coming next during a game. He had a real sense of humour, and put his dog on his visiting order. He told the screws that he had ID for the dog, and he regarded it as one of his kids. They didn't have it for a moment.

In Belmarsh, I saw heroin. I'd never seen it on the street; my cousin and loads of the workers took it, but I had never wanted it anywhere near me. As a kid my nan had made Jo and me watch a film called Christiane F., all about addiction. The scene where she was getting clean put me off heroin for life – not Jo, though.

I was in a three-up, and one of the other prisoners, Rob, was hunched over in the corner, gouging, they call it. He had a tenner's bit of brown – about 30p's worth on the street – and a silver tube, and booted it. Then he sat scratching himself all night.

There was one naughty thing I did in Belmarsh. I used to sell my piss. They do a lot of drug testing in jails, and my piss was valuable for people taking drugs. That was why A-Class got moved from Belmarsh. He was in there at the same time, though I hadn't seen him in ages. His mate on the outside was a gear head, and he put a syringe in a shoe box while out of his nut one night, dropped the box off to A-Class's dad, and his dad sent the box in without looking inside. Back then, you would get called up on a Saturday morning to get your property. That morning, A-Class got called up and they found the syringe. He was taken to the block, then shipped out.

They sacked me from the bins after the rope incident. I got a job in the workshops, and was happy to be working again. I was working away, packing tea bags, dried milk, sugar and jam into breakfast packs. One morning the screw opened my door and said, "You're out to court today, Sales." I thought, *Am I, what have I done now?*

While I was in the block, Lynn's mum had passed away. I assumed I was going to Lynn's mother's funeral, but because of the skipping rope thing they weren't telling me, for security reasons. But it turned out I'd been done on a driving charge that I didn't even know about. Being in jail, I had never received the letter. Now I was going to the magistrates' court in Camberwell. After that, they moved me from Belmarsh to Brixton prison.

As soon as I landed there on C-wing, I got a telly. I thought it was a special privilege, but everybody had one there. They put me in with a yardie who played chess and cooked the best jerk noodles ever. Perfect bang-up for me.

Later, I applied for E-wing, which comes with a special privilege: working in the officer's mess. It's outside the prison walls. Even though I'd been an E-man in my previous jail, the screw who interviewed me believed me when I told him I had no desire to escape. I'd even written a seven-page letter to the ombudsman, who sent me a reply saying even though it was the harshest sentence he'd seen, he still believed the prison had acted reasonably.

I made it onto E-wing, which was a dorm room, really. They had food we could cook, a TV room, and we got a passport in the morning to go out into the officers' mess. My workmate in the mess was Gary, a trusted painter on a four-and-a-half-year sentence, and this was the first time he'd been out of the jail in three years. As soon as we got there, he said, "Go in the toilet, wait 15 minutes. I'm off."

"Serious?!" *Don't make me complicit in that.*

"Bruv, I been away for three years and I need a bunk-up. My balls are like donkey size."

I understood. "Good luck, bruv."

Not long later, the officers came in. "Where's Gary Furley? Where is he, Sales?"

140

"He went to the toilet."

They locked down and sent me back to the wing. He'd just walked out the door, and he had his missus waiting there in a car. She picked him up and they fucked off.

As it happened, my cell was above the reception to E-wing, so I used to see all the new bods coming in, and I'd greet them.

Three weeks later, I saw Gary coming in through reception. "Was it worth it, bruv?!"

"Absolutely, it was pukka! Me balls are like peanuts now!"

"But you'll do the rest of the time closed."

"Ah well!"

He only had seven months left, and he only got an extra three.

I had no thoughts about escape, but I was starting to think differently. *Jail's easy, it's not scary. If I keep doing fraud, what's the sentence?* ID theft wasn't even a crime: they had to charge you with possession of a fraudulent implement, and conspiracy to defraud was the worst offence.

I got out of Brixton on a tag. When I had been out for a couple of days, Lynn went into labour, and I had to call them up to ask if I could go. They said yes, so Lynn and I made our way to the hospital. There she gave birth to Zack, my second son. My nan was there the whole time. She even guided the midwife during the delivery.

I couldn't go back to jail. I had to provide for my kids. I couldn't do that if I was locked away.

CHAPTER TWENTY-ONE

Freedom

When I came out, I had about £15,000 saved up and a few assets. The hardest part was being away from my family. Lynn and I decided while I was locked up that we were going to get married. I could come out and start a new life. We booked a holiday and decided to do it while we were away. We got married just after Christmas December 2000, in Mombasa, Kenya.

I was 25, had 2 kids and a suddenly there was a whole world of pressure on my shoulders. I was trying to be normal again. Del got me a job at Keyline builders in Canning Town. We had a small flat in Plumstead, but were overflowing in there. I was banned from driving. I used to cycle to Canning Town at 6 am, work all day, and then, when I finished, cycle to Bermondsey to work the controls in the cab office. Then Lynn would come to pick me up, and I'd do the whole process again the following day.

When I got my licence back, I grafted for three months and made another £10,000, then went on holiday for a month to Spain, with Lynn, Zack, my dad, his wife Denise, and my brothers Lucas, Elliot, and Oliver. We chilled out for a bit. I wanted to get my head together and figure out my next move.

When we got back, we realised we needed to get a proper place. So I went and rented a house for £1,400 a month in Eltham. I was grafting, but the bills were mounting up, and unsurprisingly, my income wasn't what I was used to. We now had another son, Ellis, born on the same day as me. He was long and thin, just like me when I was born, but his eyes were black. I don't mean he had a shiner – his actual pupils were black.

I was seeing my mates achieving things, and I could hear the little devil on my shoulder telling me that I could just commit a few simple frauds, steal a quick few IDs, and I wouldn't have to work so hard and would have more time to spend with Lynn and the kids. I still had my room at my nan's with the bits I had kept. I would pop in there on my way home from work once I got my driving licence back. At this time, Salty was also back at his mum and dad's. Salty had two older brothers and four sisters. His dad made sure they always had food on the table. He had known me since I was 10 years old, when they first moved there from the other end of Greenwich.

If I went to my nan's, I would always just have a look to see if Salty's car was there. One day Lynn went with her mate Joanna for a spa day, and I took Josh and Zack to see Nan. She took the kids over to her friend's, and told me to go and see Salty. She loved him, mainly because they had the same sense of humour. Like her, he loved taking the piss out of everything. I walked up and his mum was in the kitchen. I knocked on the window, just like I had many times before as a kid.

"He's upstairs, Tony. Go up," she said.

I knocked on Salty's door and went in. We sat chatting for ages, reminiscing about being kids and some of the things we got up to. I could see he was doing well for himself. He told me he and Jim Bobby were at it, and it got me thinking about crime again. As I left, I got a phone call.

A-Class had just been released at the end of his three-and-a-half-year sentence. "Hello bruv, you got any graft?" he asked me.

Funny that. It was like fate had played its hand. Time to stop trying all this normal stuff. Time to accept it: I was a born loser, but crime could change all that. *Don't fight it, just be the criminal you've been before, and you can have some sort of life,* I found myself thinking. *Just let it go and be what society expects me to be. Me.*

I contacted Sinner and told him that I was going to go back grafting if he was up for it. "Course I am, bruv, can't wait!" he said.

Bones needed to make money too. He was in a bad place. He'd just had a kid who was born with no thumbs and couldn't twist her wrists. He was out of work because he had to keep going to hospital. So I saw him and his daughter. They had no money, living on tinned food.

I started a van rental company, Hire Me Rental, because I knew that if the police made any enquiries about a big retail theft, they would try to track down

144

the getaway vehicle. Instead of looking for personal cars, they'd come to my rental company to make their enquiries, and I'd know all about it. So, I bought a fleet of vans, rented a retail unit on a parade of shops in London somewhere, and I had a full-time mechanic working for me. I only took cash, no credit cards.

TB came back on the scene, and before I knew it, Salty, Jim Bobby, Tina and Fava were back. This time we were building a real team – a small but efficient group. No messes or addicts. We were a super team, a few workers just like the old days. We were at it again.

CHAPTER TWENTY-TWO

Bristol

On one of our most notorious jollies, Bones drove us cross-country to Bristol. I'd hired half of a small hotel for us all to stay at. Bristol has a great shopping area, and is also located close to lots of out-of-town shopping centres. We had big motors, vans, and a plan for making sure we transferred the TVs and the rest of the loot from cars into vans once we were out of sight. We weren't loading up a van that was already full, because that looked dodgy. I'd co-ordinated everything with military precision.

As it turned out, we only got half the graft. I had a feeling, my sixth sense was telling me something. I said I wanted to check the paperwork. It turned out that Bones, who I had recently given the job of making the paperwork, had fucked up about half of it with typos. Typical – we had driven miles out and only just realised.

Bones had become my confidant, someone I trusted, more than the others. We had a blood bond. As a kid, only having a little sister, I had so badly wanted a brother, like all boys would. Someone to do things with, although not these types of things.

But this time I had to go off at him. Everyone has had a bit of my hot head at times.

"You better drive back and get it sorted, then be here for tomorrow morning."

He fucked off and stayed up all night getting the rest of the paperwork right.

Still, on our first day in the West Country, with only half the profiles, we had it off. Buy now, pay never! The profiles were banging. The salesmen couldn't get rid of their stuff fast enough. The vans were full of TVs and sound systems by the end of day one.

Bones got a call when he was on the motorway back up to Weston. "Bruv, where are you?"

"I'm on the motorway, why?"

"Move your arse, live-o! live-o!"

He got about five more calls or messages, and he could tell from the voice that something wasn't right, but nobody would say anything on the phone. He pulled up outside the hotel to see me and the others holding our heads, hungover and feeling sorry for ourselves.

"Where's Sinner?"

I told him. "Bruv, we went out last night… Sinner's nicked."

We'd been out with a lot of dough on us, because we'd cleaned up. Some guy in the club was getting lemon, coming around us, antagonising us. There were a few of us in the club. I told this guy who was looking for trouble, "I'm going to take you outside and spank you in a minute, fuck off!"

The geezer was lagging. He wasn't worth ironing out,

and I could do without getting nicked. Sinner was going mad, though. He wanted to smash this guy all over the place. I told Sinner to calm it.

We drank our drinks and left to get ourselves a kebab. While in the queue, I was squirting the sauce on, when the geezer from the club walked in.

Sinner said, "I'm gonna do him."

He felt like the guy had disrespected me. Sinner was an angry young man then, with loads of pent-up frustration, just like me. He had been bullied, and that turned him into a bit of a nasty fucker when he got going. He didn't stand for any shit. This guy had overstepped the mark, and Sinner wanted retribution for the liberty.

I ditched my kebab and grabbed Sinner. But instead of using me as a barrier, he pushed himself off me to pivot, using the momentum as he went, and lamping the geezer twice as hard. The guy was out cold on the floor, with a broken jaw, chilli sauce all over the place.

I saw there was a CCTV camera. "Let's go!" I shouted.

We were nearly at the hotel, slowing down, when we saw lights flashing behind us. Sinner said, "That's for me."

Tina, Fava, A-Class and the rest of the team came out from the hotel to see what all the cop noise was about. I was aware of the team, and what could happen to them if they tried to intervene, or if the Old Bill started nosing around them.

I turned and said to Sinner, "You're going to have to take one for the team here."

The police rocked up and cuffed us, straight away, no talking. These were country coppers, but they were acting like London Old Bill. I should have known, really – there were parts of Bristol that were just as bad as the worst parts of London.

I said, "Excuse me, why have you cuffed me?"

"There's been a report of ABH. We've been given your description."

"But I didn't hit anyone, officer. My friend got into an argument. The guy kicked him and he retaliated. But I actually tried to stop it."

"Oh yeah," the cop sniffed. "And what are you doing here?"

"I'm running a conference on fraud prevention."

That was the first time I'd ever used that line, and it wouldn't be the last.

Sinner said, "That's right, officer, I was stupid. My boss didn't do anything."

"Oh, he's your boss?"

Social engineering strikes again.

They uncuffed me, and nicked Sinner. The next morning, they bailed him to go back in a couple of weeks. He got two years for that one when he was sentenced.

We all went back to work the next day – even Sinner was there. We picked him up from the cop shop at 9 am once he'd been bailed. Today we were hitting diamonds.

I knew a geezer who wanted as many as we could get. I had two guys – one for diamonds and one for watches. I had a geezer in East Lane who bought every Rolex I ever got. I met him in Dagenham Market, selling counterfeits.

I said, "Reckon you could sell real ones?"

"I can sell as many real ones as you can get, boy," was his response.

Our plan was to hit consecutive jewellers, getting the same diamond on finance from different branches of one particular jeweller.

When we got to a shopping centre just outside of Bristol, we went through our usual ritual. First, everyone has a poo, because adrenaline's pumping. Then I did my walk around. On this particular day, I was just not feeling it; there was something in the air. My sixth sense was telling me that something was wrong. Every criminal I have ever met has a sixth sense. I guess it comes from anticipation of the negatives in that person's life. It just makes you think a little harder in these situations.

Tina went into the jewellers' as I sat outside on a bench, taking over from Sinner as the team captain. I had benched him and told him to think about himself. Tina had a scout around the glass cabinets, chose the one we wanted, and gave them the paperwork. But I was watching the business, thinking, *Something's not right, the salespeople are conferring and showing each other something.* I couldn't see what it was, but things didn't appear to be going smoothly.

So I called Tina and told her, "I think they're on us."

She said, "They're beautiful in here, darling. I won't be long, and I'll be home to give you dinner." It was code for *You're just being paranoid.*

Fava slipped in and tried the same trick for the same piece of gear. He was shifty, more suspicious. He gave them his paperwork for the finance agreement, as Tina had. We were just waiting for it to be accepted or declined. While that happened, I went in to listen, while the others were out having a fag.

The staff didn't say anything, which was weird in itself. They were not even talking to each other.

I told Tina and Fava that I thought something was up.

They both said, "No, it's just you. Everything's fine."

It was our greed taking over. This was our opportunity to walk away, but we didn't.

They went back in to collect the goods, but they'd both been rejected. Fava came out, and as Tina was leaving, I was in the Haagen-Dazs parlour having an ice cream. I saw that they were being trailed by two security guards. I gave them the eyes to say, *Don't acknowledge me, walk straight past!*

Fava can be thick at times, overly confident. If he had a good day, he would come out of a shop saying, "It's all chilli sauce, bruv!"

I was giving him all kinds of facial cues as he walked past. I called him to tell him he was being followed.

"Hello, sweetheart," he said as he answered the phone.

"Security are on to you and Tina. I don't know what the fuck's gone on, but I think they are going to grab you."

Security quickly caught up with Tina. "Excuse me, miss, can we see you for a minute?"

Fava had passports, driving licences and fake credit cards in the car. He had the key to a vehicle that would lead to a treasure trove of evidence.

I said, "Tell them you have a dog in the car. They will have to escort you out to it. Just leave it open."

"I don't have a dog, Hotts," he replied.

They don't know that, do they? People only know what you tell them, don't they?" I said.

"Clever cunt you are, Hotts," he replied.

The guards had caught up with him too. "Come with us."

Fava did as I said, and it worked perfectly. 15 minutes later, I emptied the car. I could of course have just pinged the window, but in that car park it would have been too hot.

That move was essential, because it meant they couldn't be done for conspiracy; the Old Bill couldn't prove that they had gone there intending to commit fraud. They could say they just found it and were trying their luck. And that's what they did.

We always covered for each other like that. If somebody got nicked, you cleaned up after them. If they had the car keys and you couldn't get in, smash the window. Burn it. I wouldn't have cared if it was a Ferrari. It was worth less than my freedom.

We came back home, and that weekend I decided to go out on the piss.

CHAPTER TWENTY-THREE

The Yacht

In addition to the bank tellers, we also had an insider feeding us profiles with credit scores. That way we could cream off the best ones for when we wanted something big, like a Rolex or a yacht. Rollies more than yachts, to be fair – but one time we had been on a boys' weekend down to the English Riviera, Torquay.

We rented a place, had some drinks, bit of sniff, a good old party and a laugh with the boys. As we were bowling around, I saw a boat showroom near the harbour. They were selling yachts. I saw all the pictures and thought I'd have a go at that. The one I wanted was a Sunbeam, the most expensive one in the window. It cost £890,000. I was excited as we drove back down there. It was a big move.

We were discussing whether to sail it to Spain, but I barely know how to use a compass – the ones used to sail seas are a bit different from the ones I stabbed prefects with back at school. We'd have been like Uncle Albert in *Only Fools and Horses*: "Which way to Amsterdam, Del Boy?!"

I was dressed really well, and I had a red-hot profile – a high-net-worth individual. Even when we went away on holiday, we'd take them with us in case the opportunity arose – what if we came across a Ferrari dealer, or in this case, a yacht showroom? I pulled up in an ML Jeep wearing D&G jeans with my Rollie on – not just any, but a bi-colour Daytona Rolex with a gold and platinum face, extremely rare.

The salesman was a posh bloke with blonde curly hair, and he clocked the watch. That was a good sign: he knew how to spot wealth. I sat down in their lovely comfortable showroom. There might have been an aquarium and some free wine. I chatted with him and said, "I really like that one, it comes recommended…"

"The Blohm & Voss?…"

"Yes."

"Have you sailed before?"

I was an experienced swimmer, but I didn't know anything about sailing. I hadn't thought about who I could get to be the designated captain, because I wasn't that far ahead, but we'd need somebody with a captain's licence. My uncle and dad were into sailing, so I could put one of them down, or I could just hire a captain from the marina. So, I told the guy I'd get a captain and a crew to sail it for me. That was what all the Wall Street boys did, wasn't it?

I sat down and went through the contracts with the salesman, and he listed all the paperwork I needed to bring in to confirm the credit agreement. That wasn't a problem: whatever personal documents he needed for this profile, I could make them. I told him that I would come back. It was a long way from London, but it was worth it if I could pull this one off. I returned and gave him all the paperwork that he told me I needed. But before I could sail it, I also had to come back with insurance. *Fucking hell, what am I going to do now? I never thought of that!*

How was I going to get insurance for a yacht? My brain was working overtime. Then I remembered someone had a book of Norwich Union cover notes. When I looked at one, I thought the gods were smiling on me. There was a little tick box that said "Boat". Result! I got one of these cover notes and wrote it out according to the details of the boat. At the same time I was socially engineering the geezer, phoning him to say, "I'm busy this week, but I'll be down at the weekend to finish it all off." He thought I was some *Wolf of Wall Street*-type character, and knew how these new-money bods rolled. He did not seem suspicious of me at all.

At the weekend I made my way back down to Torquay for the third time. I was sitting in the sunny glass conservatory about to seal the deal. I saw the salesman look at the cover note, then he went out the back. "I'll be back in a minute," he told me, saying he needed to make a phone call. This wasn't that unusual, because finance often had to be signed, sealed and agreed before they let you leave with the goods. There were many T's to cross and I's to dot.

Torquay is a town that runs down the cliffs, and the entrance road was visible from the showroom, very close to the waterfront. I saw the Old Bill coming down into Torquay with their lights on. *Hummm,* I thought. He has been out there a bit longer than I would like.

"Mate, I'm going out for a cigarette." So I went out into the car, lit the cigarette, and started the car up. The cop car was approaching. I wondered where it was going to turn. I edged my way out of the driveway and pulled out just as they were coming into the showroom. I drove straight out and drove home. *Ah well! I live to fight another day!*

CHAPTER TWENTY-FOUR

Here's Johnny

There was a guy from my area called Robert Bleach. Robert was a doorman working at a club called Flaunt It, just down by the Thames. He was also another statistic of crime: single parent family, bullied because of his race. His childhood had given him a great mind for crime – all the tools he needed to survive. Just like most of us, he had the right combination of poverty, trauma and abuse. He is now serving 31 years for murder, but that's a different story and not mine to tell.

I went for a drink in Greenwich. I was at The William when Robert walked in. We had a good old natter with Charlie in the toilets. I told Robert a few things about what I had been up to. And he said we could be of use to him.

He wanted to use us to go and rent properties to grow weed in. This was long before it was a popular thing to do. People did it, but not on the scale Robert was talking about. He would cut me in on all the profits if I could supply the houses. Robert had this bloke, Johnny, who was a stick-up guy.

He'd have it with a pen or with a gun, Robert told me. "We don't have to worry, they will protect it all."

I didn't know him – he was just a mate of a mate. He didn't look like he could protect himself, let alone industrial organised weed factories.

I said, "Ok, I'll think about it."

A few days later I was at home, lying on the sofa, when the phone rang. "It's Johnny. I need to see you."

So I met him on Blackheath at night.

"Robert got nicked."

"What? What for?" I ask him.

"I did a wrap-up." Johnny had gone to a drug dealer's house. He had tied up the occupants, but he had got the wrong house – he had wrapped up straight goers, so it had all gone Pete Tong.

Uh-oh.

"I left a knife on the side and it's got our dabs on it. Rob's been chored for it," Johnny told me.

Three days later, he wanted to see me again. He was a car nut, Robert, a connoisseur, and he rocked up in Rob's M3. That was a bit strange, because Robert wouldn't lend his car willy-nilly.

"Get in, I've got to go to Walworth Road."

I got in and glanced at the back seat. Johnny had a piece of artwork in the back from whichever rich guy's house he had done. A Bang & Olufsen stereo, some high-tech bollocks. He said, "It's Robert's, and I need to go and pawn it." He wanted me to be there to see how much he got for it.

"Fuck all that," I said, "I don't want that hassle. I don't want to be involved."

"Please," he said, "come with me, you can be my witness for what I've sold it for."

Eventually, I agreed to go with him. He got the cash out, but I could tell it wasn't enough. Something had gone wrong for this Johnny geezer, with this wrap-up job. I reckoned they owed somebody a lot of money – first the weed farms, now wrap-ups. It all seemed a bit desperate.

"Listen, he says, if you've got any bits of work…"

"A bit of the F game?" I asked. Fraud.

"Yeah, I'd love a bit," he said, rubbing his hands together.

"Done any before?" I asked him.

"Yeah, I've done a bit of kiting." Cheque fraud.

A couple of days later, I had a few moves lined up. I called Johnny. "You ready?"

"Yeah, mate, where we off to?"

We set off over to Essex. I did a couple of bits with Johnny, and I could tell he'd done it before. He was the nuts at it. He had a posh voice he could put on and he looked the part, so he could do much bigger jobs. I started taking Johnny out on a regular basis.

What we were doing was far from petty, small-time crime. With one TV, retail price £3,500, we could sell it at half the knock, for £1,750. Most days I had 10 TVs – that's £17,500 just in TVs alone.

Then, on my day off, I was at home and Robert rang me from jail. "Bruv, have you got that little cunt Johnny round you?"

"Yeah, he's been grafting with me."

"Listen, he's gone to my mum's house, gone into my bedroom, and he's nicked my stereo and my artwork and all my clothes. Bruv, listen, you got to graft him and get him to pay me back. I am in big shit here coz of this cunt. Please work him and give some money to my missus!"

It's hard to say no when a man is in jail, especially when he has a wife outside. He knew I wasn't going to stick drugs up my arse and bring them to him on a visit – he had other mates for that. But he needed my help. Johnny had fucked him, so I said I'd try to get Robert back some of the money this little snake had stolen.

The next day we were going out again. Salty had fucked off to Africa for a bit, A-Class had been nicked, and Sinner was in love. Just like I had many times, he was trying to be normal, trying to fit in, got himself a girlfriend, and they had been partying, so he didn't come out with us. "I'm fucked, bruv", he told me on the phone, in a voice deeper than the mid-ocean rift.

So Bones, Growler and I picked up Johnny and headed to Surrey. It was like a family affair, but we had Johnny with us, talking big and telling me how many robberies he had done.

On the way to a retail park in Surrey, Johnny asked if I could stop, as he needed the toilet. When Johnny got out, Growler tapped me on the shoulder.

"We need to chat. Johnny's pipin' crack."

He explained. "I don't know about all that robbery stuff, but I went to score the other night and he was in there, bruv, I see him. Pipin' like there was no tomorrow. Giving all the birds rocks."

Wow, I thought, *I would never have guessed that one.* It was good to have information about people who were working for me and what motivated them. It was important to understand that in order to get the best out of them. Just like any CEO, I wanted to get the best out of my workforce.

The way to manage addicts is a little different from corporate HR, though. The art is to ration their rewards. Give them shit identity profiles to work with in the morning. If they get a £10,000 watch first thing, they'll want to go home. We might be out miles away with the rest of the team – loads more to be made – but they'd only want to get back home and pipe it. So, I deliberately gave them the weaker profiles, the ones I knew less about, where they couldn't earn as much. I made a guess as to which profiles were bad ones, based on the name and the area. I had got a feel for it.

So, on this sunny day there was me, Bones, Growler and Johnny. We were miles out of London, and we'd smashed the granny out of this retail park. We'd got everything, from plasma TVs to Rolexes. I was divvying up the cash on the way home and I gave Johnny his cut, minus Robert's payback, about 10 grand.

But something wasn't right. There was an Audi following us. I clocked it, and Bones said I was just being paranoid, but I didn't miss things like that.

Johnny leant over to me and said, "Bruv, do you know anyone who can squash debts?"

"What?" I shrugged. "Not really, bruv."

I did, but I didn't want to get involved.

Johnny then started up again. "I got a problem with a geezer called DD – he's a big fish."

I knew who he was. He'd robbed one of my captains, TB, back when he was an international drug smuggler.

"If I don't pay him back, he's going to burn my mum's house down. I've got 24 hours."

"How much do you owe him?" I ask.

"Seventy grand."

"Wow. What for?"

"I took a box of white off him and piped it."

Seventy grand's worth of crack on his own! Growler told me this guy had the hunger for it so bad, he'd hide in the cupboard for two days and bug out.

I could have thrown him out of the moving vehicle right there, but I didn't. I stayed calm. "Ok, let me see what I can do." We were earning money together. I wanted to protect him.

I decided to ring my mate Exit, to see if he can help out with Johnny's problem. He worked with a firm of yardies, and had told me one night, "Anyone fucking about, we go collect money from them."

I called him. "What's happening, T?" he asked.

"Listen, bruv, one of my workers…"

"You're working again?!" There was surprise in his voice. The last time I'd seen him, we'd been handcuffed by the Old Bill, and I'd talked our way out of it.

"I need your help."

"Anything I can help with, bro."

162

I told Exit the problem with Johnny.

"Give me five minutes." Three minutes later, he rang me back and gave me an address. "Listen, you have to go there now. This is a serious one."

As soon as he put the phone down, the Audi revved right up close to our bumper. And he stayed there on our tail all the way from Reading to the scrapyard in Lewisham.

Before we go any further, I'm going to have to tell you about my mate Exit, and how I became involved with him and this bunch of yardies.

CHAPTER TWENTY-FIVE

Meet the Yardies

Bad Rass was an assassin. He knew how to work with the darker energies. Exit was tight with him, and Rass endorsed Exit to a crew of yardies in south London who were involved in all kinds of dark criminality.

To a Jamaican in the homeland, the term "yardie" is offensive because it's a stereotype of a Jamaican bad man. In those days, they were political assassins. "When we say where we come from, we say our 'yard'," Exit told me. "In the 70s and 80s when these men were bringing ganja over, the officials didn't know what it was, so they could bring it in suitcases and say it was only a herb."

Exit was an athletic gym goer, and he didn't mind being called a yardie. Back then the Lewisham Borough was one area; the crews knew each other and the top man. But now it's all divided – postcode wars and all that.

At the border of Peckham and New Cross, behind Millwall, that's where the British crack epidemic started. The Jamaican boys went to visit their family in New York and came back knowing how to wash coke and turn it into this super potent and addictive new drug. They made crazy money, and then they went to jail in Operation Harriet. Exit saw it and was wise enough to stay away.

We were at a mutual mate's house, Gravy the music producer. Exit gave me a cheque. That's how it started. He'd figured out you could go into shops with a purchase order and pay by cheque. A purchase order was something a company needed to obtain goods. If you needed a computer for your business, you created a purchase order and that meant you could go into store and pay with a business cheque. Because it was a company transaction, no guarantee card was needed, just the purchase order. Very slick!

He had a postman. "Exit, I have seven books for you," the postie would say. They were shaped the same, so you could tell it was a cheque book in the envelope. With cheque books, the higher the numbers, the more trustworthy it would be, because the company had cleared that many cheques already. Most were limited companies, and Exit didn't give a fuck about them. He'd been nicking from companies since he worked as a runner in the offices of a Savile Row tailor when he was a teenager.

When we were at Gravy's, I said I wouldn't mind some of that, so Exit gave one to me and said, "These cheques are precious, and very valuable – it'll cost you a grand". Either way, I owed him a grand, and I knew that with the people Exit rolled with, you had to pay what you owed. It was kind of a test. So, I went out to a Cash Converters, came back, and slapped five grand in his hand. The next cheques I got for free, and I would go on to have many successful business ventures with Exit.

At this point Exit was also "doing the rounds", tapping people up for money. Anyone who was into crime could get tapped up, and they would have to pay. He was a kind of general in this hierarchy of yardies. He wouldn't burn somebody's house down, but some of the other guys definitely would.

As we pulled into the wreckage yard in Lewisham, everyone was getting nervous, because these were the kind of places where the yardies did things their own way. It was behind corrugated iron gates, next to a railway line. There was an "office" in a caravan, and a yard with old car parts and tools. It was where you'd imagine a film like the Chainsaw Massacre might be filmed.

As we were pulling through the gates, Johnny said, "I don't suppose the geezer's name is Big Man, is it?"

Oh my god, I'm thinking. *Can this get any worse?* "Yeah, it is."

His arse melted then. "Ah no, bruv."

"What do you mean, 'ah no, bruv'?!"

"I owe him three grand as well."

I gulped, and switched off the radio. That same Audi had pulled in behind us, and these Jamaicans had got out. "That's him," Johnny said.

The sheer size and presence of him was frightening. Big Man by name, big man by nature. Back then, he dressed like an army bod with dreadlocks, and he had these huge biceps bursting out of his t-shirt like anacondas. And it wasn't just him – it was a car full of them, and they all got out with guns.

These guys were a bit like the A-Team. They got sent round to deal with other gangsters, and they only took serious contracts from other high-ranking criminals. When somebody heard that these boys were on the case, it was a definite incentive to get your shit together. And then there was Exit. He got out the car smiling.

"Yes T, what's happening!"

As I walked to the scrapyard's office, I could see through the door of a hut that they were putting up plastic sheeting. That was never a good sign in a situation like this. I had shorts and flip-flops on – I wasn't expecting to end my day meeting one of the biggest names in south London. Exit asked me if I wanted a zoot, flicking the lighter, and this other guy Big Man was sitting in the background, quiet and menacing. He soaked it all up, staring, a proper dark enigma.

"Alright, T, let's cut to the chase," Exit said in this voice he uses when he is being cryptic. "Where's Johnny Rotten?"

"He's in the van."

"Go get him."

As I came out, Growler poked his nose out of the sliding door, looking to see if there was any trouble – not that he would have been able to do anything about it. The team were starting to get really worried in there, speculating like an old mothers' meeting. Johnny's teeth were chattering, he was that scared. I didn't think there would be any benefit in bringing him in in that state. I went back to the cabin and told Exit that I'd talk to Big Man on his behalf.

"T, he owes DD seventy grand. Big Man's taking care of that for him."

Big Man pulled up a chair then and I felt the gravity of the situation. He could kill me quite easily.

"Who are you? Why should I believe you?"

It's funny. You plan for all sorts of things in a situation like this, but then one question takes things in a whole different direction. I had only come to see if I could help Johnny, and now I had to justify myself to this guy, while sitting there dressed like I'd just come off the beach in Miami. This was a real test of my social engineering skills.

I took a deep breath, paused and said, "Look, the geezer's outside crying his eyes out about his mum and dad's house being burned down. I know you're a serious guy, and that's going to happen. But is there any benefit in doing that? I can get you the money."

That pricked his ears up.

"What you gonna do, burn his house down and then what, kill him?" I continued. "If he's dead, he certainly can't pay you back. Nor can he pay DD."

Big Man said to me with a smile, "Alright, it's on you, then. I want 5k just for gifting you the time."

Now I had to deliver the 70 grand, plus five, just because I had had a chat with this guy for Johnny.

"You've got two weeks."

"Ok," I said.

I knew it wouldn't be that difficult to raise the cash. I had to make sure Johnny was ok, so Robert could get paid back and not have to worry that much while he was away. We dealt with it quickly. Two days. Rolex, Cartier, Rolex, Cartier, and a Bentley.

I came back with a suitcase full of notes, a carrier bag full of weed and a set of car keys. Exit had always called me Cherry, because I always added a topping. I said, "That's yours, and that's yours as well." I'd bought Big Man a present – a brand new Volkswagen Golf. It was outside in the yard. "That's how I roll, bro, thanks for giving me the chance. That, to me, is a piece of paper." After that, Johnny disappeared and Robert got 10 years for the robbery, though I don't think he was even there!

That took me to the next level with one of the biggest, most respected and feared men in the underworld.

CHAPTER TWENTY-SIX

The Great Car Robberies

A few years before, Jim Bobby, Salty and I had got a little flat in Hastings. We were looking through the local paper on a Saturday morning while a football show was on. An advert said: "CARS Take Away Today!" It had pictures of all the cars in the dealership... "All On FINANCE," the ad said.

"Go on," said Salty, "get it if you think you can." He was always like that, pushing me from the shadows, seeing how far I would go.

I rang the number. "Alright, mate? What do you need to get a car on finance?"

"Driving licence, utility bill, bank statements."

"Anything else?"

"Yes, you need your work information." I thought to myself, *I know more than this guy.*

"Can I give it to you over the phone?"

"Yes."

"Brilliant."

I went in and test drove a Mercedes, all in some geezer's name, and said, "I'll have it. Let's do the paperwork."

I sat down with him. He gave me the form and said, "You just need to sign that," then he disappeared out the back to ring it through quickly. He came back five minutes later.

"That's all approved with the finance company, sir."

"That's great. I can just take the car, yeah? Just like the advert says."

"No, we have to take that car for an MOT now. So you won't be able to have it until Saturday." Today was Tuesday, but I was going to Florida on the Thursday. Lynn was pregnant with my fourth child at the time, Abbie, a girl after three boys. I couldn't catch a later flight, as I was the only one who could take the boys on rides.

I devised a plan. I told him that I was going away on urgent business, and my mate was going to come and pick it up for me. "My PA will sort it all out for you," I told him. I called up Boots, and she called them up and sorted it all. That allowed Jim Bobby to collect it while I was out in Florida, sunning myself in shorts and flip-flops.

I took Lynn and the kids to Disneyland, anxious about whether the car was going to happen. I was there on the Tower of Terror, but was scared by the thought of Jim Bobby getting nicked.

Then the message came through. The deal was done. I'd got the car. It was like winning the World Cup. I spent a fortune with my nan, my sister, who was also pregnant, Lynn and the kids, enjoying the profits from my ill-gotten gains. Not once did I think about the poor guy whose identity I had just stolen. It was all about me.

I just didn't see it. Back then, it was just paperwork to me. I couldn't see the person. It didn't ever feel like I was harming someone.

Going through everything that I had, I had convinced myself that what I was doing was not bad. *It's only ID, it doesn't matter.* But of course I was just covering everything up from myself, turning a blind eye to my own insecurities.

On 31 March, my daughter Abbie arrived, my fourth child after three boys. I felt so lucky not to have missed the magical bonding period with my only daughter.

One day after our run-in with the yardies, Salty called me and said, "I've got a car showroom. I think the geezer is sweet."

Finance is finance, lenders will lend on anything, and most of them are all the same – same pattern. It can be just as easy to get a Porsche as it is to get a Rolex, so why shouldn't we have both? I went along to meet this car dealer. Spider was a typical Essex car dealer. A bosh boy – "bosh bosh bosh" after every sentence. Salty had been in there and the guy had spotted that he was up to no good. Spider approached Salty, and said, "I can do them all day long if you're serious? That one's gone through, bosh. Get some more and come back." Cars were always a good way to hit a profile for big dough – I learned that early on.

I went in, and standing there was this proper Essex wide boy who thought he was hard. "Who are you, then?"

"It doesn't matter who I am. Let's just do proper business together. I'll bring you as many of those things as you want. But if you play the game, I play the game."

"Yeah?" he says.

"Yeah, you just take the money, I take the cars."

He looks at Salty. "Is he ok? You ain't Old Bill, are ya?"

"No mate, I ain't Old Bill. Only thing I want is to nick is those cars outside. You in?" Salty shot back in response.

I could see the pound signs rolling around his eyes. Of course he was in.

We absolutely smashed it. For the next few months, he was doing well, selling a lot of cars! The sun was shining for Spider. I was getting on with life, going down for a smoke now and then with the Big Man. I went there one day, and he said he had some cars coming in. He knew I was into it, because I had given him the other motor. I told him about this guy Salty and I had cut in, Spider the car dealer.

"What's he giving you for the motors?"

I said, "He is giving me the cars," thinking Big Man misunderstood, but he hadn't.

"You know he gets money, don't you?" Big Man pointed out.

"From the cars, yeah," I said.

"What, he gives you these cars, and you have the right to sell them, and that's it? Listen, I love you a bit more than that, Mr T. Take me down there. This geezer's taking the piss out of you, I ain't having that! Where is it?" he asked.

I looked at him, a bit puzzled, but told him the location. I wanted to see what he was thinking.

"Take me down there, let me talk to him, straighten him out a bit. I'll bring Exit," Big Man replied.

I told him that I had to go there the next day to collect some cars. So the next day, Big Man and Exit came with me. I went in, and they stayed lurking in the background. Spider saw these two and came out onto the forecourt. "Hello, can I help you?" he asked.

"Wassup!" Big Man spat onto the forecourt. "We heard you're the one taking the piss out of my pal."

There were two other guys just inside. They heard what Big Man said, and came out.

So now Spider and the two geezers were getting a little brave. They must have missed Big Man's arms, dumb dumbs. Thinking they were hard, he said to me, "Who is this? This your boss? …Shall I call my boss?"

Big Man said, "No, he's my mate and you're taking the piss out of him. Call who the fuck you want, shall I smash you all up and then just take all your cars, how about that?"

"P-P-Pardon? What's this about?" Spider replied. The gravity of the situation had begun to sink in.

"He's coming down here with all the paperwork, getting rid of all your stock, making you a fortune, and you're not giving him a cent for that? How about you keep the cars, you get rid of them, and pay us a little extra?" Big Man explained.

"Oh no, I can't do that. I wouldn't make no money from them then; I would be doing it for free."

Spider was looking stressed now.

"Alright, here's what you can do. Tony, come here. How many cars have you had from him?" I added it up. "Right, now you're going to pay him for each and every one of those cars he's taken from you. He's making you a millionaire. And you want to treat him like a cunt. That ain't happening anymore."

"I'm not paying it," Spider replied, trying to be brave he said. His mates didn't want any of Big Man, but he hadn't realised that yet.

"Listen, I know how far this can go. I don't come second to no cunt. You're going to pay him. As for your little henchmen, they know, they can see it, I ain't scared of any cunt. We can be polite, all work nicely together, but there's a part of me you don't want to find out about. Tony's too polite, but I'm not, I am a big black silverback. I'll snap all of your necks, how about that?"

Big Man looked at me, then back at Spider. He continued.

"We're going to have some food. You can sort us out for that, and when I come back, you're going to have an envelope with something in it for us."

This was a test. Had Spider really got the balls? The underworld is full of the best social engineers – criminals have always used fear to control. Fear of violence or the promise of sex are two things that can make a man do what you want him to do. All you need to know is which the situation calls for. Fear was Big Man's specialty. He had done this to many big-name gangsters and underworld figures.

Big Man knew this, and he knew he was willing to go further than the next man. That gave him a great advantage in situations like this. He was never afraid to back up the threat.

Spider gave Big Man a tenner for the meal. Big Man ripped it up and threw it back at him. Shocked, Spider's arse was going now. He scraped around his wallet and handed over a few twenties with shaking hands.

We went out for the nicest meal we could find with this guy's money. When we went back to the garage, Spider had a fat envelope full of cash for us.

"This is how it's going to be from now on," Big Man said. "If you get X amount, he gets Y amount..."

He wasn't saying a figure – instead, he was measuring the cash with his fingers, and they were long.

We knew that if he ever got nicked, Spider would sing like a canary, so we made sure we knew where he lived. We would regularly pass by in one of the motors he'd given and paid us to take when we knew he was at home. We'd beep and shout, "Oi, big head!" But even if he did sing, he didn't know anything about us – our names or anything. If the Old Bill ever stopped me, there would be nothing to see, because I'd have all the legitimate paperwork.

What would happen when someone I sold a car to got stopped by the police? It happened many times, and they gave all kinds of descriptions of me: he's got blonde hair, he's got one leg. The people buying them from me knew where these motors came from. They were all part of the same extended network you might call the "underworld".

Another time, I sold Exit a Porsche. Unbeknown to us, it was on security watch, so he got nicked for it. Even worse, when they searched the car, they found a chopper in the back, so they did him for that too. But he had a bad boy solicitors. They came down and asked, "When did you buy that car? Two weeks ago? You've never been in the boot, have you?"

That was when we started getting the baddest cars as well. I had Jaguars, and I gave them to everyone in the manor. S-Types and R-Types. Bones was rolling around Woolwich, taking his daughter to hospital in a Jeep. All the motors were brand spanking new, top of the range. We passed them around like joints. Rolling round in the summer in convertible Mercs, big Audis, Range Rovers, Ml-500s with PlayStations in the back.

Spider told us the finance company was being rinsed so hard, it was about to go bust. So, the week before they went pop, we put 250 applications in. It was such short notice that I didn't even have buyers lined up for all the motors, but I had figured out a way of getting them off security watch. Security watch is an alert on the HPI system that tells the police there has been some sort of dodginess going on with that whip. I thought to myself, *How do they know I haven't bought that car out of Auto Trader?* If the car was advertised, that was evidence to back up your story. So that's what did. I put ads for the cars in car magazines. That way, they could have been bought by anybody.

HPI is a credit check on a car that gives you its history. It tells you if it's on finance, and it costs you £20 to search the database. I figured out that the best thing to do was to front it and say, "I bought that car, it had a smash, I put a bumper on it, and I've got mechanics who can say it's been done. We have the paperwork to show for it, including all the receipts for the money I spent on it." How could anyone dispute that? That car was now HPI clear, and I could sell it for the full amount. It had never been in a crash, but I told the authorities it had – it was proper cash for crash.

Working with Big Man would bring lots of opportunities to make money. Big Man commanded an army of guys, and an army always needed to be fed. That pressure alone always led to more criminal opportunities. Most criminal firms have a money man, someone who can cook the books and create little scams that generate money. Everyone contributes to the pot, and everyone worked as a team. Big Man hadn't really done this up to that point, as they were more the enforcers – but I was about to change all that.

CHAPTER TWENTY-SEVEN

Mortgage Fraud: A Mexican Stand Off

I'd figured out how mortgages worked when I got my first one at 17, and I'd been through the process a few more times since then. When you are buying a property, you apply for a mortgage from the bank, and once that clears, the offer is accepted, and the funds are released to a solicitor.

Mortgage fraud happens in lots of different ways, but the best way is when you get a dodgy solicitor and then you change the details on the paperwork to theirs. He then gets the funds from the bank, and fucks off back to wherever he came from. He has to do this multiple times on multiple properties to make it possible for him to retire, and he can live like a king for the rest of his life.

I'd cultivated a source in a mortgage company called Stephen. He was a posh city boy who loved girls and sniff. If you hang around Farringdon, Chancery Lane, or Soho, you meet people who like it when you can get them into a nightclub because you know the bouncers, or when you can sort them out with the finest Peruvian flake. Well, our Jamaican boys were prone to a party, and Big Man knew every doorman in London. We struck up a conversation with Stephen: "You'd like to get into that club VIP? Interesting. We wouldn't mind getting into your club VIP..."

Stephen's job was to collect mortgage offers that his company received every day and distribute them to the other members of staff. He told me this one night while I was treating him to a nice lap dance at one of the clubs in Farringdon. I'd figured out that if we changed the existing lawyer, the buyer's lawyer, on those documents, then we could redirect the funds to our solicitor, and run off with the cash. We didn't need surveyors; we didn't even need to give ID. We could just get this geezer to change the names, and the bank would send our guy the money instead of the buyer. He would then transfer the money to us, take his cut, and away we go. None of that raising mortgage offer rubbish that so many fraudsters talk about – this was me cutting to the chase, getting it a lot quicker and a lot less expensively.

Two of these mortgage offers, the ones I first changed over with Stephen, came to £650,000 combined. I switched them over to my lawyer, a Pakistani geezer in Shepherd's Bush, who was going to draw them down. I was going to do more of this stuff, build it up, and then retire. That was the plan. But on the day it was all about to be drawn down for the first time, I had been at my mate's house and spent all the previous day getting out of my head on the sweetest Moroccan hash.

Big Man was trying to get hold of me, because there were complications. There was a middleman with connections to dodgy lawyers named Wilson. I'd given Wilson 10 of Stephen's mortgage forms to place with bent solicitors. But instead of doing that, he'd sold these mortgage offers to another firm in East London.

I called our lawyer in Shepherd's Bush to check we were still on for this payday, but his secretary said he wasn't in the office today. He hadn't come in. They couldn't get hold of him. That was really odd, because it was a very important day. So I convinced her to get his home address. She had seen me a few times, so knew that I knew him well. I went round there and his wife told me he'd been missing since last night. I gave the secretary a basher number and told her he'd better call me as soon as possible.

I talked to Wilson. "What's going on, bruv? We need to get this sorted. Otherwise I'm going to cancel these payments." I could do that at any point. It only took one phone call to the banks. That would kill it for everybody. Also, was this cunt really going to split with £650,000? Was that all he was worth, when we could take millions?

Then my phone rang. It was the solicitor. He sounded terrified. "Meet me at 11 in Shepherd's Bush."

I went to meet him, and I took all the guys from the yard with me. Something wasn't right. I met him in

Starbucks at the shopping centre, and he looked really rough, like he hadn't slept all night. His tie was all skewed, and he was shaking.

"Mate, what's happened?" I asked him. "This don't look good."

He told me another firm had kidnapped him. They wrapped him up and demanded the money. The lawyer said these guys were adamant that it was their deal.

"Oh yeah? Give me their number," I replied.

I called the other firm, and the geezer at the other end of the phone line started shouting straight away.

You're not talking to me like that. I locked the phone off.

By the time the phone rang again, I was in the car with the yard crew. This firm was talking about us taking their stuff, saying they were going to shoot us up. They said to meet us at Redbridge roundabout, in Essex. There was a pub at the intersection. The geezer stupidly said, "We've got guns."

If you're dealing with idiots, that might work, but he was dealing with us. Everyone here had them. The Dread was a real madman who kept an AK47 in his house. This was no joke.

We took the A406 all the way round and back out to Essex. There was carful of us now. Big Man had made calls and there were yardies joining from all over the gaff. Big Man was driving, I was in the front, and Mad Lamar was in the back, laughing like a hyena. He had his piece hanging out of his waistband like he was in the Wild West, and he had a big dirty plunger on him.

We got to a huge intersection with a flyover. Big Man went and stood in the middle of the roundabout in the pissing rain, for three hours, waiting for them. We had cars dotted about in lay-bys. They were definitely staking us out, trying to find out how strong we were.

While I was sitting there smoking weed, this geezer came up and asked me to wind the window down. He said in a cockney accent, "Alright mate, don't suppose you know where the golf course is, do you?"

"Ain't got a clue. I'm not from round here." I wanted him to know, *I know who you are, and I know you have come as a scout.*

Lamar then said, "Look, there's loads of 'em! They're coming up the road!" He was dead excited.

It was just Big Man and Lamar at first, but the rest of the crew swarmed into the middle of the road. Bobby B, one of the crew, was going mad in the street. We were showing them that we weren't scared, and had come for war . It was a stand-off, two armies confronting one another on the outskirts of nowhere. There were loads of us now, and not many of them in comparison. If they came with guns, they didn't get a chance to pull them out. Lamar marched straight up and stabbed their main man in the stomach. I grabbed the geezer by the collar and dragged him into the pub, threw him a towel. He was getting queasy.

"Where the fuck are my mortgage offers?"

"They're here, they're here," he spluttered.

All the others outside had been dealt with. Bobby B had them all lined up against the wall like they were about to face a firing squad. Big Man and Lamar came into the pub. Lamar was in the guy's face: "I'll stab the blood clart, yo, me a plunge him Tony!"

"Leave him, Lamar, he's already fucked."

This so-called bad boy who was going to shoot us a little while ago was now crying. He said, "Please, Wilson sold us them, it was only when I tried one that they told me you can't change it twice in 48 hours." He gave me the mortgage offers, apologised, and said it had been a mistake. We left them there bleeding, with their reputation in tatters.

The first lawyer ended up stealing all the money from us and the other firms, so we never got that £650,000. He thought I was just a white-boy fraudster and he was smarter. He didn't realise I'd been through many moves like this before. But he still screwed us all over and he got away,. Bolted. It taught me a vital lesson: lawyers might run away.

We ended up kidnapping lawyers to ensure they wouldn't do a runner. The night before payday, I had Lamar turn up unannounced, with a knock on the door in a leafy suburb.

"Yo, Tony sent me!" he would say in his deep Jamaican accent.

I'd get a call. "Tony, there's a man at the door who says you sent him."

"That's right," I'd reply.

"W-w-why?"

"Because you've got a lot of money coming your way, this guy's sticking with you. Lamar will be good to you.

Put him up, treat him well, don't try to fuck us around, and all this will be sweet, you hear?" *Simple.*

The Dread would turn up with an overnight bag – toothbrush, dressing gown, the lot! Sometimes I'd send him over a few days before, and he'd spend several days shadowing them. Once we did that, they all came through perfectly. Mortgage drawdowns became really easy once Big Man and I implemented the "sleepover policy".

I carried on grafting with the guys. Having Big Man as a mate made me feel a little more confident on the street. After all, I had seen him go up against everyone who'd stepped up to him. We made some good money from those jobs and lived a high lifestyle, going on holiday all the time, having fun. Living in big houses with all the latest shit – football pitches and swimming pools in the garden. All off the back of others' misfortune. It was bad money. I just spunked it. I saved the money I had earnt legally whenever I had a job, but the criminal funds were to make me feel better about myself – strange but true. Those funds didn't last long, though. And before I knew it, TB was back with a new worker called Gollum.

Salty and I decided to hit the shops again. By this time, all the boys had become experts in finance, how the credit system worked, documents, and what to look for when something wasn't right. Getting nicked will do that for you. At court, they always have to tell you how they caught you, or a witness says exactly what they were thinking when they spotted the mistake on the ID docs we used. All the information that gets given away to us in situations like that added to our experience. Every mistake we made we would learn from, giving us a superhuman ability to spot things that others just couldn't see. Or so I thought.

CHAPTER TWENTY-EIGHT

Nicked Again

Salty had been away for the weekend with some girl, and on the way back he spotted a shopping centre outside Sheffield. He got really excited. "There's centres all round, bruv, it's pukka!" he told me.

Without checking it out first, we arranged to go on Saturday morning, the whole team. There was a convoy of three vans. I was driving one van, Salty was in another, and TB and Gollum were in another. We had made up these vans especially for this side of the business. They had signs saying "Removals" on them, and a dodgy 0800 number that was always engaged. To the outside world, it just looked like we were removal men.

In Sheffield town centre, it wasn't going well. Nothing was going through, because the profiles I'd chosen were shit. Most weren't eligible for credit. I got £1,500 in a department store, but that was it. Everyone else flopped.

So we started asking around town, "Where are the shopping centres?"

"Oh, you want to go to Meadowhall, love."

We got there, and blimey, there was every kind of retailer we were interested in, from Vodafone to Bose. *Pukka, let's go!* We did the routine.

We were getting so many tellies – two vans were full by 12. We were almost done. "What do you want to do?"

"There's Rollies here," Salty said.

"TB, Gollum, time to get the watches now," I responded.

Gollum went in and got a £7k Cartier. TB went in and it took ages for the paperwork to clear. Gollum went back to Alders.

I was talking in a Scottish accent to the girl behind the counter as I got a TV from her. I said, "I've just come down here for a wee minute shopping. Can you help me?" If I was going to pull any moves, I had to pretend to be from somewhere else. All the team had used a cockney accent, and I didn't want to be associated with the crew. You don't get that many cockneys in Sheffield, and they'd all bought the same model of TV on credit.

A guy like Sinner might stand out, but it's more about what people see. People in shops aren't trained to know what an ID looks like, or a document. They always look at things through straight eyes. They were more worried about building their commission than checking for fraud.

Gollum went to get another telly after the Cartier. The stupid cunt. I'd told everyone, 42-inch tellies. All the others were on special and too cheap – we didn't want them, we wanted the latest ones.

He calls me when he's inside. "Alright bruv, I've got the 50-inch."

"For fuck's sake, bro," I said. "I thought I said 42-inch?"

"The box is massive. Can you come and help me? Cheap, though – it was only £1,750."

"That's why I told you to get the 42-inch, you thick cunt!" I told him.

"I can't carry it on my own. Please come and help me, Hotts."

Because he'd bought the 50-inch one, and he was only a little guy, we now had to go and meet him. This went against all our protocols. But I was feeling over-confident and thought they were a bit sleepy up here. We had had a good day.

So I headed to meet him. I ducked all the cameras getting over to him, and as soon as I put my hands on the TV, the Old Bill was all over me and Salty. Not as silly as we had thought, those northerners. Gollum had also called TB, but he was not coming – smart really. When Gollum got the telly, the girl at the counter had made the call, saying, "There's a load of guys been in here from London today, and they've all bought tellies. Is there a coachload of them up here shopping or something?"

That one slip took the whole operation down. In the end they only got me, Salty and Gollum. One van got away with all the goods, and the other two got impounded. Both vans were full of goods that we had grafted that day.

CHAPTER TWENTY-NINE

Interrogation

I was sitting in the cell, waiting, until finally they came to get me and took me to the interview room.

The first words out of the cop's mouth were, "You're going to get five years for this."

They were trying to fluster me, make me think I'm fucked!

"What for? I'm just a driver, I drive a van. That's it," I replied.

They were having none of it. I'll never forget the duty solicitor. As soon as I went into the interview, I started talking. I wouldn't normally do that, but I was being cocky. They asked me silly questions, like, "When you were driving, what were you listening to on the radio?" The Old Bill do this to set the scene, then if you are lying they can catch you out with little details.

"Dire Straits, Money for Nothing." I was so cocky, I was about to burst into song.

"So why are your prints on this?"

The Old Bill had dusted down all the documents – licences, utility bills, and credit cards they had found in my van. TB had sat and watched all of it, because he didn't have the keys when I'd gone in, similar to that time with Fava. This time, though, we hadn't had the chance to empty the vans of its ill-gotten gains. That was a massive mistake for us that led to a treasure trove of evidence for the prosecution.

My solicitor advised me to make a written statement. It said I was there, but I was just the driver of one of the vans. I had just been paid as a driver. I was stalling, really. I wanted to see what else they had on us. I knew they were going after us for conspiracy to defraud, the most serious fraud charge. They didn't charge me on the day, though. They gave us a date for us to come back.

Six weeks later we were back in Sheffield. They put us straight back in the cells. This didn't look good. The PC came down and though the flap in the cell door she said, "I hope you're proud of yourself."

I still wasn't having it.

"Proud of what?" I quickly shot back.

"I've got a lady upstairs crying her eyes out because of what you've done." I could only see her eyes as she glared at me.

"I never stole any lady's ID." I was confused now. *That's not what I do.*

"You stole her dead dad's identity. Your dabs are all over it." She slammed the flap shut.

I felt like someone had just kicked me in the stomach. It was my first true realisation that there were victims to the crimes we had been committing.

At that point, I knew I was fucked.

I will always be grateful to that officer. She made me wake up to the reality of what I was doing, and for that, I will always be sincerely grateful. She got commended for her work in catching us, and she should be proud.

They only got three of us. TB saw it all unfold while he was walking to meet Gollum. He saw the Old Bill and just slipped into the food area. He sat there and watched us get nicked out of the window. At first, we thought they didn't know TB was there. In the interviews, though, they showed us all a picture of him, and asked us who he was. They put a warrant out for him, but he was already long gone by then.

My lawyer tried to get the charges knocked down to aiding and abetting. I played along with it. But then they said they wouldn't go for just aiding and abetting (which is a lower charge): they wanted me on conspiracy. They suspected I was a ringleader. They had Salty as the number one, and me as number two. They had phone records, text messages. There were pages of texts on the phones for Ikea, Argos, Currys – orders from people requesting stuff, complete with the order numbers of the goods they wanted. And they had all the receipts.

The policewoman was blonde and quite good-looking. I was dressed in Versace jeans, £500 shoes, and a Rollie on my wrist. We walked in and she was waiting there. I cheekily asked her, "Where is your partner?"

She replied that her colleague thought this case was a pile of shit. "He thinks it's too much work to nail you guys. But I don't."

I knew then that she'd be going the whole hog. They had loads of shit on us, although it could have been worse. We'd been nabbed before, by one of the huge retailers we'd been whacking for months. They sold household items, a global brand, and we were clearing them out one time. I was in the store, and I could feel that we had eyes on us. Then my team started disappearing one by one off the shop floor. Suddenly I got swarmed, but not by the Old Bill: the store had a private security firm on us. The shops hired a team of specialists to come in and find whoever it was that had been targeting them, and that was us. They gathered all the team up, took us into a back room and showed us the fraudulent transactions covering a period of months. "You have hit us for hundreds of thousands," they said. It got so tense, I thought at one point they were going to iron us out. Then one of the security guys said, "This is a warning."

I said "A warning? Where are the police?"

"We are not calling them. Don't ever come into our stores again or we will call them," they said.

We never went back to that store again. When I go in there now to buy bits, I get a nervous feeling in my stomach. I'm looking over my shoulder the whole time.

The after-effects of crime are something I had never considered.

Sheffield was different, though. I had touched all the paper-work, stored in a secret compartment in the van, and they'd found it. There were over 100 driving licences, utility bills, and credit cards. They also had over 100 insider credit reports from a referencing agency.

The police in Sheffield had found loads of receipts. There was one for a washing machine I'd got from somewhere else. They saw it was in Enfield.

The female officer said, "You've been doing this all over the country, haven't you?"

They went to House of Fraser and Alders, looked at all the fake accounts, went to the people we had impersonated, and got them to sign statements denying they had made these purchases. I never in a million years thought that they would link it all. I had massively underestimated the police.

At that point, I knew I had to plead guilty. They had us. I'd been to prison before. It wasn't that bad in there, so I know that if I went guilty now, at the first opportunity, I could limit the damage and get a lesser sentence.

Conspiracy is a really serious charge. But it was only one count. They were only doing me for that one day's looting of Meadowhall in Sheffield. One count of conspiracy to defraud doesn't look that bad on paper. When you get charged with a serious offence, it goes to the magistrates' court first. They couldn't deal with it there, though, because conspiracy is a Crown Court offence. At

Crown the first hearing is a case hearing, where the judge hears the case. Then it's pleas and directions.

At that point, I pleaded guilty. Gollum also pleaded guilty, and Salty pleaded not guilty.

Once I'd pleaded guilty, they released me on bail, and I had to report to a probation officer, who asked me a load of questions and prepared a pre-sentence report. I was quite naive to think that I could mug them off, because they clearly weren't buying any of it. I clearly wasn't ready to take full responsibility for my actions at that time, and was still looking to pull off another escape:

PRE-SENTENCE REPORT
Tony Sales
DOB: **/**/**
Age: 31
Offence(s): Conspiracy to defraud 05/06/04
Court: Sheffield Crown Court
Date of hearing: 14/02/05
by Andy Burston, probation officer

1.1   This report is based on one
interview with Mr Sales at Bexleyheath
Probation Office.
1.2   Mr Sales was co-operative throughout
the interview process.

2. OFFENCE ANALYSIS
2.1 Mr Sales has pleaded guilty to an offence
of Conspiracy to Defraud committed between 1
January and 5 June 2005.

THE BIG CON

2.2 The circumstances of this offence are that shop staff at House of Fraser in the Meadowhall Shopping Centre, Sheffield became suspicious of an individual, a Mr (Redacted) [Gollum], who had purchased a television having obtained credit up to the value of £3,250. Security staff concerned about this transaction alerted the Meadowhall CCTV team and asked that this man be monitored to see where he went and whether a car/van registration number could be obtained. CCTV cameras observed this individual make his way towards a van, and police from Meadowhall Retail Crime Unit were alerted. An officer then approached three males, who were at the van, indicating that he believed the television had been fraudulently obtained. Mr Sales and his two co-defendants, Mr (Redacted) and Mr (Redacted), were then arrested. Further enquiries then revealed that a range of forged documents had been used to obtain a variety of electrical items and it was established that Mr Sales' fingerprints were on a number of the fraudulent documents. Having been arrested, Mr Sales initially in interview denied any knowledge of the offences and the in second interview, provided a "no comment" response.

2.3 In discussion with Mr Sales about the offence, whilst he has pleaded guilty, he says this was very much on Counsel's advice and he maintains that he knew little of the fraudulent activities that were occurring. According to Mr Sales, he had received a telephone call from an acquaintance asking him to take a van to Sheffield for which he would be paid £200. He said he did not ask any questions about this, as he was out of work and needed the money. Having arrived in Sheffield, he was told to meet Mr (Redacted) who he knew at Meadowhall Shopping Centre. Having arrived there, Mr Sales admits he knew "something iffy" was afoot and suspected it was to do with fraudulent cards/accounts. He says he found a holdall in the van with a number of false identifications and utility bills. However, he says that he wanted the money for the day's work and so he remained in the van while Mr (Redacted) went into the shopping centre. I asked Mr Sales whether he knew about any other fraudulent transactions and he denied this was the case. "I was driving the van. I cannot account for what others get up to." It was evident, despite lengthy discussion, that Mr Sales' viewpoint regarding the offence was not going to change, he being adamant that his was a peripheral involvement, albeit knowing that something illegal was occurring.

2.4 I enquired as to whether Mr Sales had considered the impact that this offence would have on the victims, namely large corporate stores and the victims whose identities were stolen. Mr Sales maintained that as he was not really part of the obtaining of the fraudulent identities, he could not really comment, "but I guess they wouldn't like it, I know I wouldn't." Equally, he acknowledged that the companies would be "annoyed" by such crimes, but "to be honest, I did not have much choice but to take the van up there, I needed the money." I asked him, when he indicated that he did not have "much choice," whether he was pressurised into becoming involved with this enterprise. However, Mr Sales says this was not the case, indicating that when he referred to "not much choice," it meant in relation to his financial position and the need for money to support his family.

2.5 My own assessment of this offence is that there is substantial evidence to indicate that Mr Sales was involved in this conspiracy despite his assertions that he did not play a significant role. The evidence suggests that the offences were pre-planned, Mr Sales and others deliberately targeting Sheffield for these frauds. Mr Sales is adamant that this is not the case, stating that he only visited Sheffield on that day and he was not fully aware of the extent of what was going on. However, my view is that this explanation lacks credibility and that Mr Sales needs to put some considerable thought into his behaviour if he is to avoid future offending.

I knew at this point that Gollum and I were bang to rights. I just wanted to limit the damage to the sentence. As a worker, Gollum was automatically placed at the bottom of the conspiracy. That was why Salty and I had always said we were just the drivers. This meant that we would be below the team if anything ever happened, as it now had.

3. OFFENDER ASSESSMENT
3.1 The court will notice that Mr Sales has one previous conviction of an entirely different

nature to this current matter. On 14 February 2000, he was convicted at Basildon Crown Court of an offence of Possession of an Imitation Firearm with Intent to Cause Fear or Violence, receiving a 15-month sentence of imprisonment. Whilst I have not been able to obtain details of this offence, I understand it relates to an incident at a nightclub in Southend. Mr Sales says he got into an argument with staff at the nightclub and foolishly returned to his friend's car, where he took out a blank firing pistol and threatened door staff with it. Mr Sales went on to add, "It was a very stupid thing to do. I have no excuses for what happened that evening."

3.2 Mr Sales was born and brought up in the Greenwich area of London. He recalls a difficult childhood, his parents separating at an early age and Mr Sales being brought up primarily by his grandmother. As a consequence, he says he lacked any stable family environment and at the age of 13 or 14, due to his disruptive behaviour at school, he was sent to a special educational support unit. Whilst there he received one-to-one tutoring, which he says was beneficial, leaving school at 16 with both literacy and numeric ability, although no formal qualifications. Following leaving school, he says he went to Erith College, but left there and went to work in a clothing store. He remained there for some four years before again changing employment and becoming a taxi driver. He was in this employment when he committed the firearms offence. Following his release from custody, he gained work as a taxi driver, this time for his father. However, he says he could not make sufficient income from this employment, so stopped work. At present, Mr Sales is unemployed, although he says he does undertake the odd driving job and has tried to gain employment, as yet without any success.

3.3 In discussion with Mr Sales about his use of drugs and alcohol, Mr Sales admits that he is a habitual cannabis smoker and also takes cocaine on a regular basis. Mr Sales says he started smoking cannabis as a teenager and states that he would find it hard to stop using the drug, despite the illegal nature of this behaviour. In connection with his use of cocaine, whilst he says he is not dependent on the drug, he admits to taking it frequently. However, he does not link this usage to his offending, maintaining that it is purely recreational and that he can stop this usage if so required. With regard to Mr Sales' use of alcohol, he admits to drinking heavily on occasions and being prone to binge drinking. "When I start, I sometimes find it hard to stop." I enquired as to whether he thought his use of alcohol was problematic for him. However, Mr Sales after some thought said this was not the case. It is also perhaps worth noting that Mr Sales' offending, in my view, would not appear to be directly drug or alcohol related, these offences in my opinion being committed to fund Mr Sales' general lifestyle, which incorporates drug and alcohol usage.

4. ASSESSMENT OF THE RISK OF HARM TO THE PUBLIC AND LIKELIHOOD OF RE-OFFENDING
4.1 An offence of this nature will clearly cause the Court concern. [...] Mr Sales did nothing to

THE BIG CON

curtail his co-defendants' activity, and my
view is that Mr Sales was a willing participant
in this enterprise. I have little doubt that
the motivation behind the offence was financial
gain, Mr Sales using the money to support his
family and associated lifestyle, which includes
the use of drugs and alcohol. Yet in my opinion,
he is unwilling despite the guilty plea to
accept full responsibility for what occurred,
and to that end it would be my view that there
still remains a high risk of similar offending.

In terms of the likelihood of re-offending, that
probation officer was bang on. Because three weeks later,
while out on bail, I got nicked again – with TB.

TB needed money to fuck off to Morocco. The Old
Bill pulled us over near Fenchurch Street station in
the City of London, and I was sniffing Charlie like a
hoover in the car. When they took me to the cell, I took
the powder from beneath my ballsack, and carried on
sniffing it.

They hadn't found that, but they had found TVs,
credit cards and documents in the car we got nicked
in. We were going to sell all the stuff to some geezer in
North London – one of TB's mates. He had said he'd get
more than I could for the goods, and he needed as much
as he could get.

We had had two cash jobs as well, taking money out
of the bank without any inside help. If you don't have
a bank insider, you can get somebody to be a money
mule. You write a cheque out to that person and as long
as it clears, the second it does, you get the person to

draw out the cash and give them a cut. TB had a couple lined up, so I went back to Exit and got a couple of his specials.

I hadn't seen him or Big Man in a while. As I was leaving, Big Man told me he wanted to talk to me.

CHAPTER THIRTY

Keyser Soze

"There's a guy called Stanley who came to me as a debt,"
Big Man told me.

My mate Ginger took Stanley to a solicitor once to
help him out, and when they walked in, the solicitor
recognised Stanley and said, "Blimey, you brought
Keyser Soze with you. This guy is the ultimate super-
criminal." He was nicknamed after the character in *The
Usual Suspects*. But Big Man preferred to describe him as
a "little trouble-making cunt".

Big Man warned me about him. He said, "He'll trick
you and fool you, he's so clever. He can manipulate
people into giving him everything they have. He's a
magician, is Stanley."

Stanley was short, with a limp – hence Keyser. I felt
kind of sorry for him. He was very clever, and claimed to
have worked at the highest levels of finance. He knew all
about the most intricate deals, the markets, and how to
launder money and make numbers disappear. He could
bamboozle people with his logic.

He'd always robbed other criminals. It often boiled down to hare-brained schemes, but because he was so slippery, he got away with most of it. On this occasion, he'd set up a mortgage deal, telling a load of underworld people that he could launder money for them, when he couldn't. He stole all the deposits, totalling £140,000. A classic advance-fee fraud that for some reason many got suckered into. This time, though, he had chosen to fuck with the wrong people.

Big Man asked me if I would keep an eye on this guy. He would pay me to do it, as he had another firm paying him to sort out all the drama Stanley had caused. With all the other stuff going on, I thought it was a good time for me to get back into the shadows. TB was sorted and had his money to go, so why not?

Stanley had convinced this crew of underworld figures to invest in something, used it to put a woman in a penthouse, and now had big-name gangsters wanting to fuck up his life. They'd gone to his parents' and put it on them. But, even though it was risking his and his family's life, Stanley was still playing games with them.

These other gangsters had said, "Can you do us a favour, Big Man, and keep an eye on this gentleman?"

Because they hadn't harmed him yet, he'd given them a date when he promised he'd produce the money. It was convoluted, but his parents would have to remortgage their house to save him. Big Man wanted me to oversee it all and make sure the transaction all went smoothly.

Stanley settled himself in and got comfortable with all the yardies. He was becoming part of the furniture, sharing the lifestyle. Big Man had to tell the firm not to get too close to him, but to remember he was a job. Big Man noticed how Stanley was starting to get into everyone's head. Certain members of the crew were doing a few side deals with him. He had this art of befriending them and making them think he could help them. Once he was in their heads, they became less concerned with the transaction he should have been doing, and more concerned with what he had promised them.

I kept asking him what was happening, just like Big Man had told me to, but he even spun a story to ease the pressure from me. So I was at home, thinking they were just getting on with it. I had my own stuff going on, so I wasn't that bothered.

They were down the yard one day, and the boss of the other crew rang the Big Man up.

"Big Man, are you about?"

"Yeah. I'm down the yard."

"Is Stanley there?" the guy asked.

He was. He was sitting down with the firm, having a meal he'd been to get them from the takeaway. Big Man looked over. "Yeah, he's with the crew."

"Big Man, you don't understand what this geezer is doing to you. He's messing you about, he's lying to you," the other guy told him over the phone.

What Big Man didn't know was that there were some geezers from the other firm outside the yard, ready to storm the place and take back Stanley. The other crew had been in contact with the parents, a respectable elderly couple. They told the crew the money was going straight into Stanley's account. What Stanley didn't tell them was that he'd received the money weeks before, and he'd already spent most of it. He only had about £20,000 left.

While Big Man was on the phone, the other firm came into the yard. They stormed straight in. They must have planned it like that, so Big Man was nowhere near Stanley. But lo and behold, there were several of his friends, and they were armed to the teeth with shiny objects that split the skin. Although Big Man chose to use fist and foot, the others didn't.

It went badly for the other firm. Stanley had promised the money to Big Man because of what he had done with the other firm, but now he was in Big Man's debt. That was when I got the phone call to go down there again.

When I turned up, a couple of the other firm were tied up with blood running down their faces. There were a few others running away as I was driving towards the scrapyard. *What the fuck has gone on here?*

"See those two that are tied up, Mr T? They wanna fucking come to my place, and cause trouble. No sir!" Big Man said. "They think they can come in here and attack me. I'm working for them. What do they take me for, some sort of silly cunt?"

He told them, "You can go to the police, but I'll come to your houses. You've disrespected me by coming down here instead of having a conversation. You got it in your head that I'm some sort of conman, some fucking trickster. You think I won't keep my side of the deal, you think I won't deliver. This here is Mr T, and he can produce more money than you'll ever see in your lifetime. I want peace, but you've let this start a war."

It wasn't the norm for wars to break out between two big fish like this. The underworld is a very small pond, so lots of big fish always bump into each other. Normally, though, they talk it out. You can't have two big firms going at it too much. But this lot had come to Big Man's place and started trouble.

As all this was going on, I went and grabbed Stanley. He told me everything. That was the first time I had ever really smelt fear in someone. Stanley actually smelt shit-scared.

"Tone, please help me sort this out. I know you can. This lot are going to kill me if you don't help me."

I knew he was socially engineering me to help him, playing on my nice side.

"Please talk to Big Man for me," he begged. "I know we can get the money together. I just fucked up!"

To keep the peace, I said I would help. We walked back in to the caravan in the yard and sat down on the kids' school chairs.

I took a deep breath. "Look, bruv, he's spent the money."

Big Man was shocked. "What, he spent the money? I've got everything sorted out, had these cunts come down and attack me in my own place, and now you're not paying the bill?"

He went really calm, and then he gave Stanley the biggest backhander I have ever seen. Stanley's head flew back. Big Man grabbed his face with both hands and bit straight into his nose, snarling.

Stanley screamed. "No, no! I'll get the money. Please, Big Man, I've spoken to Tony, he said he can definitely get the money again. There's ways we can do it."

Big Man turned to me. "Do you want to do this?"

"Yes," I said, "but this time I'm in control. I make sure the money comes back. No one dies. I make sure everybody walks away paid."

Big Man was fuming. He went outside into the yard. Inside the caravan's front room, there was a sofa, a table, and two seats. I sat on one of the seats. Stanley sat on the sofa, holding a rag to his nose, peering at me over the top like a chad.

The Dread was skinning up this big reefer. "A-wha you say? A-wha? You say you spent the blood clart money?"

Whack! Whack! The Dread popped him with a bit of wood. He walloped him a few more times for good measure. Stanley just looked at me with a kind of satisfied smile, and poked his tongue out. He'd just had his nose half bitten off, and he was making silly faces.

I wanted to laugh, but I couldn't because of the scenario. We went outside and he was dripping with blood.

"That wasn't too bad, was it?" he said. He might be right, because they could have ironed him out completely.

Just before he went away for Christmas, we smashed Waitrose with credit cards and got so much stuff we had to use a van to carry it all away. I said to Stanley, "Give Big

Man and his boys everything in the van. That's your gift to them – it will make their Christmas."

During that time, I learned a lot about Stanley. Even though his parents were willing to bail him out, he had been through a lot as a kid. We became close. I could see that all the pain he had suffered in his life had made him this way. It gave him a crazy drive to have money, and he didn't care who he ripped off to get it. Because I had just stepped up and helped him get out of all that shit, he loved me.

He paid Big Man back every penny and then some. Stanley and I pulled a few moves together. I was always in control of the money just in case – I wasn't stupid! But he had a brilliant brain for this stuff, even if his exit plan was always a little last minute. One time Spider called me up, saying he had some travellers' cheques, and asking me to meet him. So Stanley and I met him in a pub.

Spider was carrying a black holdall. He opened it and showed me and Stanley the contents. Looking in the bag, I said, "How you going to cash them?" But I already knew the graft. Travellers' cheques were a fraudster's training ground. They were how I learned to lift and change signatures and digits, and play with the paper. When cashing travellers' cheques, the bureau had to authorise them. The teller would make a call, and they would give you an authorisation code. But I worked out that the authorisation process was fatally flawed.

Spider wanted in on the deal, but he couldn't. He was a liability. He told me that he met this guy through Salty, so I took them from him. I told him to give me the guy's number, which he did. He and I took over the deal. He was probably thinking about Big Man's biceps!

I called the guy up, and told him what had happened and that Spider didn't have a clue about these things. I told him I would be taking this over. "Give me a few days and I will set something up."

I wanted to renegotiate, though, because I didn't like the terms he'd set up – that we would cash them for 15 percent. What was that all about? I wanted in on this, but I wanted half. This wasn't a walk in the park, it was serious graft.

I went to meet them in the Justice pub opposite the Old Bailey. Their main man was there. I walked in like that, perched up, and said, "Spider is out. This is how it's going to work."

The boss had this little Indian guy with him, and he lost it. "Who do you think you are? Do you know who we are?"

"Fine." I got up and walked out, leaving the bag on the table. I got to the traffic lights, crossed over, and by the time I'd got to the other side of the road, the phone was ringing. It was them. They wanted me to come back to the meeting. The whole way through, the main man didn't say a word. He told me, "I like you. That was front. There's not many people who would know who we are and do what you did."

"I know you can't launder these cheques with anybody else," I told him. "This is a high-scale operation. I've got a way of cashing them. But it's going to take some serious graft, and you'll get your money back."

I ended up getting 50 percent of the value of the cheques, but I had palms to grease. I'd probably only get 10 percent of the value: £100,000 out of a million.

Stanley knew a family called the Attlees. They ran a big hotel in Kent. I took over a floor at the hotel and installed all the equipment needed to deal with the travellers' cheques. Stanley and I were the only ones who knew where we were. It was top secret.

We set up in the hotel, and got our crime factory running.

First, I walked into a bureau. "Hello, I'd like to cash some travellers' cheques." I took in all the ones with no stamps or light stamps, which were easily reusable, and chanced them. I did a hundred grand like that. I knew I was about to go to jail, so I just wanted to get some money to leave for Lynn and make sure my family would be ok, no matter how long the judge gave me.

Once all the equipment was in, I could then proceed onto the next stage: I filtered all the cheques with stamps on, to wash off the stamps and make them work again.. The stamp showed that they had been cashed before. That was how these guys were getting them: these were cheques from foreign tourists that had been cashed in London. I had French, American, Canadian, Australian, Indian, and Sri Lankan cheques. So I needed to have passports from all those nations, lined up and organised. I had paid £2,000 each for real blank passports. I could add a photo and had Bones – who was a real artist – draw the name in pencil. Once we'd cashed a cheque, it was just a straight-up photo and name change. I'd switch the picture for mine or one of the workers who'd go in and cash them.

It was a real logistical operation, making all those passports for all those cheques. My mate B helped make them, and he was very good technically. I had a proper laser printer, and three towers and computer screens used for different functions in the counterfeiting process.

It would take about six weeks, but it would bring in £1.4 million for the team. Who wouldn't go to war for six weeks? Tell your wife you'll be back soon with a huge payday, and she'll probably be fine with it. We would still have a party, because I'd booked the suite for weeks.

While we were holed up in the hotel, one of the other firm's middlemen called and said, "We've not seen any cash for a while".

I brought all the cheques back, and told him to poke it up his arse. Because these cheques included smaller denominations. "Are you going to make a passport for a £76 cheque?" They just didn't understand the amount of work required.

We smashed it, and just like we had promised, we gave Big Man his cut. I was always true to my word. In that world, it was all I had.

CHAPTER THIRTY-ONE

On the Run

Lynn was pregnant with Abbie, and I couldn't comprehend how I would cope with not being there when she was born, or not being around as she grew up. I told her I'd been nicked, but I said it was just to do with driving. I was driving some people, and they had fraudulent documents on them. It wasn't a big deal. She asked why they kept me for so long, and I said it was because they were questioning the others, and I had previous, so they assumed I was part of it. But I reassured her. "There's nothing to it, babe. They don't have any phone records or communications with me." But they did have all the records between me, Salty and Gollum. We weren't that smart.

My plan was that Lynn would only find out when she needed to know. I didn't want her stressed: it would be bad for her and the baby. I'd come out with it later. "Here's what I was doing... I was under a lot of pressure."

Salty had said to me, "If the trial goes bad, I'm fucking off, bruv." A day or two into his hearing, he saw how

213

much evidence they had against him, and he fucked off. When I told him about the amount of evidence they had on me, he said, "Fuck them, don't go." I had three boys and a daughter on the way. I hadn't told them I'd been arrested and was about to go to prison for a long time.

I started to think a lot about what he had said. He jumped bail, and a week later they sent for me and Gollum to appear in Sheffield Crown Court. I said I was unwell and couldn't come for that week. The next week, I claimed there was traffic. "Alright," they said, "make sure you're here tomorrow." On the way to court, I stopped off in a caff in East London, worried out of my mind.

I switched my phone off. Now it was fight or flight. I would be on the run for the next six years of my life.

They had an old address I'd given them when I was nicked, but I'd moved twice since they took me down. If I was smart enough, I could hide in plain sight. I went to court as Tony Sales, but had already changed my name a week after I got nicked. It cost me 50 quid to do it with a solicitor. So I got a new driving licence, rented a house, and opened a bank account in my new identity.

Once I figured out that the DVLA don't really check your old identity with the new one, I applied for a new driving licence and passport, and fucked off to Lanzarote with TB. We bought a three-million pound apartment as a bolt hole I could disappear to if things got too hot. It had a balcony overlooking the marina, with a seven-person jacuzzi. We had bottles of champagne and played football on the balcony. We were smoking Cuban cigars infused with Courvoisier brandy.

We spent a couple of weeks there. When I came back to London, I really hit the road.

What's the best possible cover when you're on the run – especially when your missus and kids don't know? I'd been a cab driver before, so I became a cab driver again.

To get a London black cab, people think you must have passed the Knowledge. They are wrong. All you need is what's called a badge and bill. It's just a piece of paper with different coloured fibres running through it. It's what black cabbies get when they pass the Knowledge. I sat for hours gluing fibres onto the paper, smoothing it down, making it look really nice, then dabbing it with coffee to make it look old. Then I went to Hobbycraft and bought an oval metal mould. I melted some metal into the mould and when it had all cooled, I painted it green and then put the black numbers on. It looked really good. This allowed me to hire a taxi that was insured and had its own registration number. It was now a fully licensed London black taxi, although the one I had was bright pink, with "T-Mobile" written all over it.

All I needed to do was take the badge and a bill and a week's deposit for the vehicle to the garage, and I was off, cabbing around London, flashing my lights and honking my horn! I went up to Mayfair and did little runs around. I stayed away from airports: the cabbies have a queueing system there and it all seemed a bit formal, a bit risky even for me. So instead of airports, I went up and down the King's Road. I went everywhere but an airport.

One Saturday night I made £780. Black cab drivers
have their own restaurants, and if you go in with a badge,
you get a discount. It was steak pie and all that – mother's
home cooking. Beautiful stuff! I'd go in and play the
badge-number lotteries with the other cabbies. I even
had a little black pouch, like the one that cabbies have
to keep their money in, and that was how I'd deposit my
cash into this new bank account. It wasn't as hard as you
would think to get cash in the bank!

CHAPTER THIRTY-TWO

Teething Problems

There are problems with being a fugitive. For a start, Lynn and the kids didn't know.

The way I'd sold it to Lynn was that we needed to disappear on everyone. Start afresh. She was okay with my new name, and believed there was a legitimate reason for it. Why would I tell her? She wasn't from that world, so she didn't need to know. I never did deals at home. No talking business at my house. At home I was a joker, a clown who did silly things, just like any good dad. I just wanted to be a dad like any other good man with kids. I had been damaged because my parents never did the family thing, and I would never let that happen to my children.

As far as Lynn was concerned, I was a taxi driver with some other interests. I went out in the mornings and went to the office or drove a cab. Why would she question it?

She wasn't a Prada handbag girl. Every now and then I'd try to go and kit her out. Once I spent about £850 on a pair of jeans for her – D&G with diamantes on them – but she tried them on and didn't like them.

By this time I'd been on the run for a couple of years. We had a six-bedroom house in a nice part of Chislehurst: five bathrooms, two kitchens, a swimming pool and a football pitch in the back garden. We would go away on holiday and live lavishly. The kids had the best time by the seaside. That was why I did it all. To give them something I'd never had.

But the flip side of the criminality being on the run was that I was now a sort of invisible dad. I could no longer do what a lot of other fathers could do for their kids. I tried to be normal, to fit in as if nothing was wrong. I took Zack to football on a Sunday morning, but it would get complicated when the other fathers started asking me social questions.

"Oh hello, you're Zack's dad!" they would say. "Do you live around here? Where do you work?"

Fucking hell, it's only a football match, and now it's turned into a full on investigation of who I am.

So I'd try to stay away from football and their schools, avoiding contact with the other parents and teachers. I didn't want anybody knowing who I was. Even getting to see Josh became hard. I would pick him up and we would drive back to mine. I would be all happy to see my boy, would start driving back, and an Old Bill car would come up behind me. It made my arse go every time. I don't know why I ever ran. It damaged me really badly. Paranoia set in quickly, making me think about every single move I made.

And then there were the other problems with being a fugitive. Teething problems.

After a couple of years of being on the run, I got a toothache. I'd always had impacted wisdom teeth, and they crushed other teeth when they pushed forward. I had been to the dentist when I was younger and got scared of the drill.

As I was chewing on something, I felt a back tooth break. I took some painkillers, and thought, *Fuck, I'm going to have to go to the dentist.* I rang the emergency dentist in my brother's name. I didn't have his NI number, so I had to call him to get it. Then when I got there for the extraction, they wanted all this other info. I started getting paranoid about touching the paper.

I got the dentist to take that one out, but the next one went a week later, and I didn't want to take any more chances by filling out forms in my brother's name. The police often use dental records to identify people. So I got a basic pair of pliers and burnt the ends to get rid of any germs. I stuck them in my mouth, clamped them on the tooth, and started to wobble it. The pain seared through my synapses. I got some Jameson's whiskey and poured it into the cavity, as if whiskey was going to stop the pain! I wiggled some more. Then I felt it snap. It came out with a huge root. I extracted three of my own teeth while being on the run, and did my own fillings too.

Taxi driving was a good cover to some extent, but then again, I was vulnerable in a car. If I saw a cop car behind, my arse started to twitch. If the boys in blue decided to pull me over, it was a straight choice between pulling over or a car chase. I'd never drive spot on the speed limit – just over, to make it seem like I wasn't scared. The feeling I got in the stomach when it happened was horrible, but I got used to it: my body became accustomed to stress. My whole life had been stressful, and this was just another thing I had to take in my stride.

Black cab drivers don't get stopped by Old Bill very often, but they have PCO checks. So when I went out into town, the people who regulate the cabs, Hackney Carriage, would be out inspecting. They made sure your cab was clean, you had your badge and bill, and that the meter was working correctly. You needed to be able to show them receipts.

My licence was moody, so I wanted to minimise the number of inspections. If the light was off, I could say I was delivering the taxi to somebody for an MOT. So I'd drive into town with the lights off. But then I'd go to work on King's Road and Oxford Street because they were straight roads, and I didn't need to know much except what was either side of them. I had a really good satellite navigation system called "Serious": it told me all the points of interest that a cab driver should know.

Pulling up outside the Dorchester was brilliant. The man with the hat waved me through. It was like being in a game of Monopoly. Surprisingly, I never met any criminal connections in the cab.

To begin with, I was making a living from black cabbing. But as I was on the run, to maintain that cover, I needed resources. I had a massive house and rent to pay, and I had also rented other houses all over the place and put my name on the electoral roll as Tony Sales. I flipped it. Tony Sales was now a *fake* name.

During this period, Tony Sales was supposed to have lived in Southend, Sheffield, Brighton, and a few other places. I acquired houses or flats everywhere. Most of them I rented to people I could trust, on the caveat that the Old Bill might turn up looking for me. Which they did. In Brighton they kicked the door down and left a warrant. They went to the Southend rat hole loads of times, because that was where I had my old driving licence registered. They knocked on the door and asked for me, but the tenant said they didn't know me. They rocked up at my nan's; in her house, there was a cupboard with all my old clothes in it. Even my counterfeiting equipment was still there at the time. But I'd trained her. She'd just say "No, I haven't seen him for months. He comes back every now and then." She was confident enough to do it; she knew I was on the run, because I couldn't hide much from her. I trusted her with everything.

They didn't ever drill her or any of the others at the houses, because at the end of the day, it was only one count of fraud. The copper in the City of London had told me that for the rest of my life, he'd be keeping an eye on me to make sure I was paying my bills and keeping my nose clean. I knew that I would never really escape their scrutiny.

Still, there was no point escaping jail if I was going to live without freedom, and of course, I wasn't able to live the kind of lifestyle I was used to on a cab driver's earnings.

While out one day in the cab, I got a job that took me over by one of my old pals, the watch guy. I went in to see him and he had the most amazing replicas. Rolex, Cartier, Breitling. He told me that all the insides were stamped too. They had even been sealed the right way.

"How much?" I asked him.

"For you, 500."

They looked the absolute nuts, so I told him I would think about it and give him a bell.

I headed back south, and popped in to see Big Man, Exit and the rest of the boys down the scrapyard. We smoked a few reefers. Exit and I had a couple of dragon stouts and Big Man was sipping on a Supermalt. He has never drunk a drop of alcohol in his life. I told them all about the watches after hitting Goldsmiths on credit. I knew that their pre-finance agreement looked like a receipt. So I told the Big Man and Exit that I could go into Goldsmiths and get the paperwork for a certain watch, wrap them up in a Goldsmiths bag with the "receipts", and we could sell them for half the knock of retail price. We could tuck up a few people who we didn't like. So that's what we did. Exit said he knew someone. We got a Rolex for another pal a day later, worth £9,000 in the shop.

I went to the jewellers', got the finance receipt, then gave it to Exit to sell to his link, an Indian guy who had sidestepped Exit in a previous deal. As Exit said, "The greedy always get scammed." I played the wingman like I had before for the Nigerian boys. "Yeah mate, I just got it on moody finance," we would tell them. We did a few, then while having some breakfast over in Woolwich, I bumped into Growler. He was living with my sister around there somewhere, and just popped out to score a bit of gear. He came into the cafe and I told him what I had been up to. I asked him what he was doing for money.

"Shoplifting, bruv."

I could see he was hitting the gear hard. I wondered how Jo looked. He was a handsome young man with bright blue eyes. He always looked the part. Life had been cruel to Jo. He had had so much trauma from a young age, it was no wonder he had ended up with a heroin addiction. They say that life can sometimes imitate art, and that was definitely true in Jo's case. Maybe while watching Christiane F. as a kid with me, he saw some sort of escape.

Growler told me that he could sell some of them. He had had them before, real ones, so it wasn't that hard for him to put the word out. We were mainly targeting underworld figures, as they couldn't go to the Old Bill, and that worked perfectly for me. Exit and Big Man were in, meaning we had muscle if it all went wrong. But Growler was smart, or so I thought. He knew not to let the people he was selling the watches to know anything about him, or us.

"Get me one for about 5k retail," Growler said, "and I'll get two and half grand off him." I took a cut back to Big Man and told him that I'd done another one. Growler called me to say he was up for another one – he said he had 10 grand to spend. This time I gave him two moody Rolexes and a Daytona. I told Growler, "Tell him that's a right bargain. The Daytona is rare watch and looks just like my real one."

About half hour later, Growler called me while he was with the guy. "He wants to talk to you, Hotts."

"Put him on," I said.

"Hotts, do you mind if I take these ones to my friend? He owns a pawn shop and I want to check them out, that ok? Growler knows me, he knows where I live. You can trust me."

Fuck! "Yeah, that's ok mate, but don't run off with them, will ya? I don't want to have to send the boys out," I said.

I told Growler to leave them with him and come away. This could turn bad. I knew my mate said they had all the stamps and stuff, but I didn't know that. I hadn't seen inside; I only had his word. This guy took them to his pal, and three hours later he called me to say, "Sweet, Hotts, they're good. I'll take as many as you can get."

These fakes were so good, a normal jeweller or pawn shop couldn't tell the difference.

Growler brought back the 10 grand. I told him we would have him the same again next week. This meant I didn't have to put myself at risk of driving the cab every day – I could stay at home a bit more, stay off the street. The next week we did it again, for another 10 grand. I had hit this bloke for £50,000 by the end of the month.

It was coming up to Christmas 2007. As always, everyone wants a little more at Christmas – even criminals – so I came up with an idea. I told Growler to call his guy and tell him, "Hotts has an insider in a jewellers'. The guy told Hotts he can rob the place and take all the valuable watches out of the safe. There will be about 100k's worth of watches – all the top sellers." We had a big fish on the line, and it was time to reel him in. My cut of 25k would see me have a very nice Christmas indeed.

He went for it, and a few days later the deal was done. It was a good job: I did it all over the phone and he didn't meet me once, only Growler.

Christmas came and went, birthdays came and went, and the watch money from Growler's pal became a distant memory. February came along, and I got a phone call from his flatmate Tim. He was distraught. "A guy came over and smashed Growler to pieces. He's a proper mess..."

"What's happened?"

The geezer had found out the watches were moody, and he burst through the door when he opened it. He ran at Growler, taking him down in his own home, and gave him a kicking. There were teeth and blood all over the carpet. He'd been proper smashed up.

While I was on the phone to Growler, my little sister, who lived with my mum, called me. I told Growler I would call him back.

"Tony, there's a guy here, and he's told me you have to ring him within the next 24 hours."

"What! What guy?" I asked.

She seemed scared. "He said you better call him or else."

Or else? What the fuck does that mean?

"Okay, give me the number." I called it.

"They're moody!" A voice said to me on the end of the phone. "You took a liberty! Don't be doing that with me, you cheeky little cunt. You've got 24 hours to bring the money back for the watches, or I am going to kill your mum. That will fucking liven you up a bit."

Are you mad? This guy didn't know what I looked like, and he certainly didn't know who I had cut in on the deal my side. *I'll iron you out and everyone you know, mate. I've got an army who'll come for you. You're in the game just like us, so suck it up, that's how it goes. There is no bringing mums into this without serious consequences. Are you out of your fucking mind?*

"Kill her," I said, and put the phone down. That might seem harsh, but anyone with my experience knows that you don't give someone 24 hours' notice that you're going to kill their mum. I knew he wasn't serious.

I headed straight over to the yard. The boys were armed up, suited up, ready to rock and roll. There would be no messing about. The geezer rang my phone again. It vibrated on the table for a few seconds. This time Big Man answered.

The guy was in violence mode, seething about the watches, saying mums were going to be killed over this.

Big Man waited for him to finish venting, then politely said, "Hello, mate, is that all you've got to say? My name's Big Man. Go and find out about me."

This always happened in the underworld. It's a small place, so everyone knows everyone, and if each side does not know each other, one side will know someone that will. It's better that way.

Bang. He put the phone down. The boys were ready to go. Lamer was bouncing around like Tigger. "Them say they kill Tony's mum, what da blood clart, me a kill them." But Big Man told them all to calm down. This horse hadn't bolted yet.

Ten minutes later, the phone rang again. "Big Man, I'm sorry. I'm just the middleman. Please, can we wipe the slate clean?"

I grabbed the phone, still fuming, shaking with rage. This cunt smashed Growler up. That was understandable. But saying he was going to kill my mum? That's a fucking liberty! She might not have been there for me as much as she should have, but mums and nans are held with the highest regard in the underworld.

"What you in the middle of, bruv?" I said. "You're going to get caught in the crossfire now. We're ready to go to war for this." I could tell he had turned into a pussy now – no big talk – and I just wanted to rip him a new arsehole. The underworld is full of people like this: they get brave because they know a big name.

But Big Man was a master. He gave me a look that let me know I should let him do the talking.

"You threatened to kill my mate's mum," Big Man says. "I think that's really disrespectful. So here's the thing. *You've* got 24 hours to get another fifty grand. Otherwise, I'll kill your mum."

They paid that one quick, funnily enough. 150 bags out of one geezer. Big Man's reputation would always squash beefs quick. They didn't care about any other criminals. These guys could deal with a problem when no one else wanted to. *Almost* all the time. Some things were just way too big to get involved in, though – like when Mohan Singh showed up at the yard in a white Rolls Royce.

CHAPTER THIRTY-THREE

The Cult of Power

They said Mohan Singh started a cult in America. One day he showed up at the yard in a Rolls Royce, wearing flowing robes with a harem of women, like he was Charlie with his angels. I looked at him, thinking, wow. This guy is nuts! A bearded black Buddhist with a Rolls Royce and an entourage in tow!

Mohan came into the caravan where I had my office, took one look at me, and said, "What's wrong with your shoulder?" I'd had something wrong with my shoulder for years. He yanked it about and then cracked it all into place. Whoa! I got a mad rush of blood to my head.

He'd come to us through Steven Segal, because he was the actor's guru. And our friend Alex Green was a stuntman for the film *Exit Wounds*, which Seagal starred in.

"Think about him," Big Man mused. "He came to us from nowhere, and he said we were doing good things in a bad world."

That was why he said he wanted to meet us.

In the caravan after the back massage, Mohan heard me say that my son Ellis was born on the same day as me. He asked for my date of birth. I told him. "We have the same birthday," I said.

"What date is that?"

"11 January."

He looked it up on the Buddhist birth charts, and he said: "You're a Bodhisattva – a person who is able to reach nirvana, but delays it to help others who are suffering." *Fucking hell, does this guy know me!* First my shoulder and now this. "Your son," he said, "is what we call a Bodhisattva Skywalker."

"A what?"

"It means they're sending for the new Dalai Lama."

I went home and told Lynn jokingly that our son might be the next Dalai Lama. We both remembered how when Ellis was born, his eyes were black. We thought he looked like an alien. At two years old, he was running up and down the stairs with rucksacks. Maybe he was training for something.

Four or five days later, I got a call. "Tony, the Dalai Lama is here. He'd like you to come over and see us in North London."

"Mohan, I've given this some thought, and I'm not having my boy thrust into the spotlight. I don't care if he's Luke Skywalker. I want him to know what it means to feel normal, because I never did."

"We're not joking, Tony. Your son is a really rare occurrence. We'd like to have him involved with us. He should visit Tibet with us."

"I like you lot," I said, "but that's out of the question. I'm sorry, my son ain't going nowhere!"

Mohan Singh had actually come here with a problem. Supposedly there was a group of people in America who were after him. Basically, he wanted protection from Big Man and the crew.

He had a massive place in Belsize Park, with crazy amounts of money which, according to all the stuff online, his female followers had given him. He wanted a firm who didn't ask questions about what the danger was, and would stand up to whoever came against him.

This was real power. It went to a different place, and it would be curtains for all of us, playing at the highest level. We never could have helped him.

Mohan Singh went to prison in 2010. He was sentenced to 10 years.

That was the thing about Big Man and the crew. They knew what they could and couldn't get involved in. They would always help out anyone who was suffering or being bullied.

Big Man was monitoring the street for people who might go to the police. There were always people coming in and out. That type of activity, no matter where it is, would always get attention from the boys in blue. Big Man knew it.

The police passed by the yard all the time. There were people on their wanted list like me inside too – not that they knew who I was, but they would always drive past looking to see if they could spot anyone they might be looking for. I would be in the office, and I'd say,

"They're driving past again." But they knew if they came in with so many dangerous people around, there might be a bloodbath. Even the Old Bill were smart enough to realise that was good for nobody.

That made me feel safe. It may sound strange, but at least I knew the police were not going to just come charging in. Even if they had, as the white guy, we all knew they wouldn't focus on me.

Big Man bounced out and approached them in their car. As he did, the cop wound his window *up*. Big Man banged on it. "Can I help you?"

"Yes, you can."

Big Man spoke very politely. "I know our road is on the way to the station, but I see you driving past every day. You're probably wondering about the people in there, they might be on some list?"

"Yes, we do wonder," the cop said.

"Well, why don't you park your car inside and have a look?"

When they saw him chaperoning the Old Bill into the muddy yard, everyone started scrambling around, wondering if Big Man had lost his mind. But if the police were going to pass by every day, we needed to know our friends could be trusted to keep their cool if the Old Bill barged in uninvited.

"Listen, officers," Big Man said. "If there's ever anybody you want to speak to, or suspect, come and ask for Big Man. Come and see me, and I will deal with it. But please don't just barge in here just because there's an aroma of weed. It's the medicine of the street. My people get a bit jumpy when they see a police uniform.

All the residents that lived on that road loved us. They too felt safe. No one could burgle houses on that road, because Big Man would not allow it. Every single person who went there was always respectful.

That was when I started to think about my next move.

CHAPTER THIRTY-FOUR

Radio & the Beginning of the End

I'm a pirate by nature. So, naturally, I loved pirate radio, growing up listening to Centerforce 88.3. As a kid, I got shout outs whenever I could. To be able to communicate over the airwaves is empowering. To hear the same music, and have conversations about things other people aren't thinking about.

We had a radio station in the yard, called Pure Kronix. Garage, House, Reggae, Soul, Urban – all from the street. My name was Tony Ads, because I sold the advertising. I wished I had discovered that I was good at this stuff before I turned to crime. So many kids like me end up in crime; it's such a shame, because many people from that world have creative minds, but no real opportunity to do anything with them.

We bought a container, and I kitted all the yard out with brand-new railings on the front, and awnings like they have on car washes, as a place for all the DJs to smoke. The container had plaster board, cornice, and coving all the way round, so it looked like a proper studio. We put a DJ booth in there with a wicked mixer. I spent two grand on an engineer to tweak the EQ, so it was proper radio quality.

To start a pirate radio station, you need a rig with a transmitter and aerial. You tune the rig to the frequency, and that's it, you're broadcasting. The guy we got to do it for us was the best; he told me you had to protect the rig. So we attached jacks to the transmitter box and twisted it down into a hole, then sealed it so nobody could find it – or if they could, they couldn't get it out. Then we got a horn that amplified the signal. Our tower was miles away from the studio in Lewisham, but we had a direct line, and we were on 104FM. Some nights we would get calls from listeners in Norwich. Funnily enough, Lamar was a really good DJ. Like everyone else, criminals love music.

Pure Kronix had 40 DJs, and it ran for a good couple of years. Each DJ paid us £40 – that's already £800 a week – and they liked it because it was advertising for them, it got them out there. We had a lot of big names come there two, to play, sing or just hang out.

Eventually it got raided. About 50 Old Bill came in. I thought *This is it. The game's up!* But I didn't need to worry. As the only white man, I just walked out of the back door.

But that made me realise what my life had become. Always on edge, always looking over my shoulder. Constant stress, constant pressure. And I was leaving my family vulnerable. If I had been arrested, I would have gone to prison without providing for Lynn and my kids.

I'd been on the run for six years and that had changed my DNA. I had calmed down because I couldn't afford to take risks. Now I was able to see that I couldn't make any good from that life and money, just like my nan had always said. I knew I was going to get caught eventually – it was only a matter of time. I'd had enough. I didn't want to do it anymore. It was tiring as fuck, messing with my mind. That was when I started to get guilty feelings. I began to think about how to rectify some of my mistakes. Having been selfish and worried about myself for so long, I hadn't taken into consideration all the damage I'd done to all the people whose identities I had stolen. The money just covered it up for a while, but the feeling of worthlessness was still there. The problem was, I hadn't got a clue how to go about it.

CHAPTER THIRTY-FIVE

Visiting Permission

I had become really close friends with some of the most dangerous people on the street. It's not all about work, it's about having somebody you can trust.

Exit introduced me to a guy from outside Big Man's network. His name was Ace, and he was a debt collector for some of the world's biggest cartels – a real-deal bad boy from New Cross, with connections in Jamaica, South America, and Miami. He didn't sell drugs. He knew people that did, and just like Big Man, he would collect the money that others just couldn't. Ace and I had the same sense of humour. We were both valuable commodities, but we were more like friends. He had the most amazing business brain. We met when I was selling cars we got from Spider. Back then, he would buy them off me and give them to members of his crew to drive around in.

I wanted to get on it one night. We had just sold the watches, and like always, I wanted to party after the move. Ace had told me about one of his South American white powder sellers, and I fancied a bit of the quality stuff. He and his crew didn't care where you were from or how big your name was. If you were doing illegal shit, then to these guys you were fair game.

I fell asleep on the sofa and woke up at 2 am. My phone had dropped down the back of the sofa. It was one of those big leather recliner types, all electric, so I just went up to bed, totally forgetting about Ace. I got up in the morning and rescued my phone from the sofa. Seven missed calls. Ace had tried to call me five times and Big Man twice. Shit, Ace, I forgot. I called him and his phone went straight to voicemail. I made some toast and coffee and tried to call him again. Still voicemail. I continued to call him, but all I got was voicemail the whole day.

The next day Exit called me. "Ace got nicked."

They got him on something proper naughty. They had connected him to something else he wasn't even involved in, but when they came in they found what I had ordered. I felt dreadful. He called a week later and told me everything that had happened. He was in prison on the Isle of Sheppey. Then he said he wanted to see me.

I had to go. "Bro, you know I am on the run," I said. "That's the last place I want to be." There were three prisons on that cluster: Swaleside, Stamford Hill and High Point, where Ace was.

I had my passport and driving licence in my new name. I knew there was no way that prisons would have access to the police database of fugitives. The only risk would be if a screw recognised me, but that was pretty low risk, as I had never been in High Point. I called up, and was on hold for hours, trying to get through. Finally, I booked the Visiting Order in my moody name. A week later I got to the visitors' centre. I was nervous. Here was me running away from jail, and yet here I was, willingly walking through the gates.

Ace had some cars that he wanted me to sort out. I started going on prison visits regularly once I got comfortable. I could do it in my new name, book it in and go with the ID. If they could have clocked it, they already would have done. They weren't expecting fugitives to go in through the visitors' entrance.

Going into the prison got me thinking that a few years inside wouldn't be so bad. It couldn't be worse than the limbo I was in and it would give me the chance to start again. I began thinking about giving myself up. Salty was out by now – he went on the run for three years, and was sentenced to two years and eight months when he got caught. So now I knew what the maximum sentence was. Gollum only got 18 months on probation. He was going through tests for the big C, so the judge had been lenient. I knew I was going to hit somewhere in the middle, plus time for jumping bail – but by handing myself in, I might limit the damage.

But first I had to put the rest of my affairs in order. I had to make sure Lynn would be okay, and had enough money to survive and pay the rent. I imagined I would get two years minimum after what happened with Salty and Gollum. It was August 2010, and I planned to give myself up in October. I had to wait for certain transactions to go through, because there were so many restrictions. I decided not to tell Lynn yet, because I could still get bail and see what happened.

My mates had started a kind of charity, doing something that I believed in. It was a good idea; they worked with kids like the old me, kids with ADHD or learning difficulties. The ones everyone says you can do nothing with. They showed them there was more to life than just stabbing and shooting. The two guys that started it wanted to divert them away from crime. Those two came from council estates where kids got sucked into crime, just like me. They had seen it first hand, and a lived experience is an invaluable commodity. I ultimately introduced them to the person who sponsored them. I gave most of what I had parked up, so they could help others. They didn't know where the money came from, but they knew it must be connected to me somehow, It's still going today, and those guys have changed many lives.

I had a massive bag full of phones, and I planned to cash them in. This would be one of the last things to get rid of. I was nearing the end; six weeks to go. I'd kitted out Lynn with a load of jewellery and other pieces to tide her over.

I'd arranged to meet Salty in a petrol garage in Basildon. He was already there as I pulled in. So I got out and started filling up the car. It was a hot August day, and I was in my shorts and flip-flops. I'd been smoking weed all day, and I stank of it.

As I went into the garage to pay, I saw two coppers sitting in there eating their lunch. Just my fucking luck. As I walked up to pay, I could feel them looking at me. I paid for my petrol and walked back past them, towards my little green Polo. As I got in the car, I saw that they were coming over towards me.

"Can you step out, sir, so we can have a word?"

Shit, they'll smell the weed. There were no tests back then, so I could just say that my mate who I had just dropped off smoked it. Still stoned as fuck, my brain was racing. Weed slowed me down and made me think a little more clearly – I suppose it worked like the drugs they use to control ADHD.

"Get out of the car, sir. What's your name?"

He didn't even mention that I stank of weed. I gave him the moody name I had been using. As soon as I mentioned the moody name, he grabbed my arm, and said, "I think you are wanted, sir." He then confirmed over the radio, "Two warrants". I knew that was me – for Sheffield and the City of London arrests. He grabbed my arm and cuffed me. I'd been here before and talked my way out of it. So I was still composed. But the PC said, "There's a warrant out for your arrest."

"Is there? I think you've got the wrong person." I was still trying it.

"We'll sort it out back at the station," he replied.

At that point, I knew. So I asked the copper, "Can I have a cigarette?"

"No, you can't," he snapped back.

"Look, it's going to be ages till I get to have one, so if I can't have one now I'm going to kick off," I replied.

He walked me away from the garage and let me have a cigarette.

I lit it and then sat down on the kerb. My legs were feeling tired. *Fuck! I am going into jail in shorts and flip-flops.* Then, suddenly, I felt elated. *It's over!* The copper could see this on my face and asked, "Are you alright mate? You look relieved."

Then it all hit me like a ton of bricks. Everything that I had been through over the last six years flashed before my eyes. They called in another car for me, parked mine up, and took me to the station.

They put me in a holding cell and left the door open. Through the door I could see another room opposite with a telephone sitting on the desk. I slipped out and crossed the corridor. I sat down and called Lynn. I told her everything and cried like a baby with the relief. Lynn was in shock. She stayed calm but I couldn't tell how she would react when it all had time to sink in. I must have been in there for a good hour before the copper came looking for me.

"What the fuck you doing in here?" he shouted. "You been using that phone? SARGE! We got a smart one here!"

He threw me back in the cell. "No phone call for you, you cheeky bastard."

It didn't matter though. I had finally told Lynn what I needed to.

The next morning I was taken to Southend Magistrates' Court. The warrant from the City of London police needed to be dealt with before they could send me off to Sheffield, where I had jumped bail. I thought this one was going to be worse than the Sheffield one, but by a stroke of luck, they had to deal with it quickly so they could send me back up north. I got in there and spoke to the duty; she told me that they had charged me with possession of cannabis class B, and possession of cocaine class A. No fraud charges.

"Is that it?" I asked.

"Yup, that's all they have told me," she replied. "How do you want to plead?"

"Guilty," I said. "Let's get that out the way."

I went into court and the judge gave me a £285 fine. That's a right result. If I had known that at the start I would never have run, but hindsight is a wonderful thing.

Monday morning came, and they took me in a sweatbox all the way from Southend Magistrates' Court to Doncaster. I made them take me to a service station on the way up. Handcuffed, I was allowed into a cubicle while the transport screw waited outside. I wanted to see what the processes were like, to see what the escape possibilities were, but mostly to waste time. I wanted to make sure that Lynn had time to be there. I knew it would be the last time I would see her for a while.

We finally arrived at Doncaster Crown Court. I had to wait for the judge from our case; he had put something on there that meant we had to go back in front of him. That was not a good sign! It was a relief when they led me into the dock and Lynn, my nan and my grandad were all sitting there. Lynn was smiling, but with tears in her eyes. I knew she wasn't going to do what I'd always feared, and abandon me. Fear of abandonment was the one thing that had given me most of my hang-ups throughout my whole life. My mum and dad had left me, so I always expected to be left again.

I stood in the dock. The judge said, "This will be a quick preliminary hearing. Presumably you don't want bail?"

"I do!" I said.

"Pardon?" the judge replied in disbelief.

The duty brief they had got for me came over and said, "You don't want to go for bail, do you?"

"Yeah, I do want to go for bail." I replied. "I can pay 100k in cash for security if they want?"

It's a misconception that we don't have cash bails like in America. We do. We have sureties. You pay it to the court in case you don't return. I had seen my mate Ginger T do this years before, so I knew they did it. And damn right, I wanted it. Who would choose cash over freedom?

The brief said he would say it, but all he could be sure of was getting the case adjourned so my original brief could take over.

The judge didn't like me at first. When we asked for bail, he laughed out loud. I'd been a fugitive for six years, and now I was asking for bail. He must have thought I was a right cocky bastard.

He gave me three days in the nick, on judge's remand, so they could get my original brief. Three days later I was back in court again. This time my original brief was there. His was a nice friendly face, and he was pleased to see me. He gave me a big cuddle. "Tony! Where you been, Spain?!"

"I stayed in south London."

"Why did you run?" he asked. "They classed your case the same as Ring. If you'd have come on that day, you'd have got 18 months probation."

I felt fucking sick. What did he just say?

I was heartbroken. I wouldn't even have served time. I'd just messed up my life, and gone through all that madness, for nothing.

The judge gave me a nine-month prison sentence for Conspiracy to Commit Fraud, and three months for failing to surrender. According to the Bail Act 1976, running away is only a summary offence, with a maximum of six months.

But I was honest with the judge about why I did it. I said my wife had been pregnant. As a boy who grew up without his dad, I didn't want to miss the bonding period with my only daughter. I said I was happy to accept whatever punishment he gave me for that. He respected me for that, taking it as a man, with a real reason behind it.

I was put in a private jail in Doncaster. They had Sky Sports, and that night, Man United were playing. I was messing around with my orange juice carton and I saw that it had a straw on the side, wrapped in clear plastic, stuck to the side by some glue. When warmed by touch, I could create impressions, fingerprints, in the glue. My cellmate was allowed in and out of the cell as he was a

red band – a trusted prisoner. Curious, I got him to wrap the glue round his finger, and rolled it around to get all the prints. Then I wrapped it around my finger. I walked up to the scanner and pressed it with his fingerprint. It worked. I got out.

With the knowledge of how I could just walk out the door, one night I was walking down the corridor of this A-Category jail, thinking, *That's it, I've had enough, I'm going.*

I thought I might just do it. I remembered how they punished me in Belmarsh when I wasn't trying to escape, so I decided now I was going to do it just to make them look like fools. And I wouldn't tell them how I did it. If or when they caught me, I'd just say the door was open and I was just wandering around looking for some food or a nurse. Then, suddenly, I thought, *What are you doing?*

There's this film, *I Love You Phillip Morris*, starring Ewan McGregor and Jim Carrey. One of them is an ex-copper who becomes a fraudster. I'd seen in the film how he escaped six times and got a 150-year sentence for it. It was based on a true story, and the guy was legendary, but did I want to go down the same path? Notoriety? A lot of guys in my position had the same question looming over them: *What are you running from?*

There wasn't much point in escaping. Even El Chapo

got caught, didn't he? I got all the way down to the visiting hall, and was about to walk out the doors, but then I turned back. It was the one time the odds favoured the police. How many criminals stay on the run forever? Not many. The odds were very much stacked in the authorities' favour. Besides, it really wasn't bad in there. I already had status in the jail. In this one, you ordered your meals on a computer, and I'd found out a way of getting it doubled.

There was weed and everything in there, but I didn't go near it. I did get involved in a hooch boat, though. All the cockneys got together to make hooch. We ordered all the separate ingredients on the canteen. I got the sugar, and somebody else got the Marmite, potatoes, and the rest. It was like the *Goodfellas* scene – while they were making spaghetti and meatballs, we were brewing moonshine. Once it was delivered, I gave it all to the Sri Lankan geezer, and he brewed it in fire extinguishers. Nobody knew how, exactly, but I'd clocked it. The stuff this guy made was like Vodka and orange. It was amazing.

A week before it was ready, I bought a two-litre bottle of orangeade on my canteen. I poured its contents down the sink and emptied the daily orange juice rations they gave us in a carton into the bottle. All the time this hooch was fermenting in the fire extinguisher. For 11 days we waited. All the while, I had the full two-litre bottle of orange juice on the windowsill in my cell.

We were meant to have a party on Saturday: football, betting, drinking. We were all going to get pissed, put the radio on, and do Mars bar bets. But Scotty, who was in the hooch boat, was a gearhead, and he had an argument with a screw during association on Saturday morning. He threw a TV down the stairs at her.

"Poke your TV up your arse," he told her.

So now we were all on lockdown for two days. Monday came around, and everyone wanted to get drunk – "We'll do it today, we'll do it today," they were all saying. They were obviously desperate to get off their heads.

The party ended up in our cell, and wow, this hooch was special. But I only had one shot of it. I knew they were getting louder with every drop, and I could see what was about to happen. It was inevitable. Then a screw came along past my cell. The door was on the latch. She poked her head around the door.

"Alright, lads?" she said.

Sparks, who was proper half-cut by now, grinned and laughed. "Come and have a drink with us, Miss!"

"No, you're alright," she said, pulling the door back.

"Listen," I said then. "She's going to get the others, and they're gonna storm us."

"Nah she ain't, she's alright!" he replied.

"I'm telling you, bruv. Get rid of that stuff," I warned him.

Nick, my pad mate, took the bottle of hooch out and hid it in the toilets. The others started pouring one down the sink. "What about this?" they asked, grabbing the orange juice.

"No, leave it!" I said. "I got a plan for that."

Sure enough, the screws turned up and turfed everybody out. "We're nicking you for drinking alcohol.

This is a blah-blah offence…"

I said, "You're not nicking me, I've not been drinking. No one has."

"Yeah, yeah, we'll see about that," they replied.

"Go and get the breathalyser. I'm not drunk," I told them.

They sent for the breath bag, and I blew clear. I'd only had one shot, which wouldn't affect a guy my size. I blew into it again. *There you go, green!*

They were desperate to nick me, so the female screw who had had the TV thrown at her on the Friday grabbed the orange juice. "Here, we've got the evidence."

"Fair enough," I said. "Let's see at the adjudication."

In private jails they don't have SOs and POs. They have managers and senior managers, because it's more corporate. This senior manager, who'd got two pips, called me in. It was the same deal as in Belmarsh with the skipping rope: the screws wedged me in from behind. This time, though, I was dead calm, because I knew I was going to fuck them.

"How do you plead?" the manager asked brusquely.

"Plead to what?" I ask.

"Making alcohol," he replied smugly.

"I haven't made any alcohol. Not guilty," I said confidently.

He reached behind him and put the bottle on the table. "I put it to you that that's alcohol."

"I put it to you that you haven't tested it," I said cheekily.

"Pardon?" he looked puzzled.

"That's pure orange juice. You give me it every day in a carton. The bottle is from my canteen. *What* are you nicking me for?" I said, tilting my head and squinting my eyes.

He unscrewed the lid and smelled it, before passing it to the screw who nicked me to sniff. They were fuming. And Nick, my cell mate on trial with me, started laughing.

"We'll sort this out," the manager said, and stormed off.

Weeks later, we were playing pool on the wing, and it came up in conversation. "Bruv, that was super smart thinking," said Nick.

I smiled. "It's all about playing chess – having a plan in place if it all goes wrong. By putting a diversion in place for them to latch on to, we can cover our arses. Common sense, bruv, they expect us to be stupid. We ain't!"

The manager came back onto the wing with a nicking sheet. "Sales!"

I laughed at him when I read it. Now they were trying to charge me with making orange juice. That was what it said on the sheet. Technically, it was a breach of prison rules; like brewing alcohol, it could go to an outside court, and you could be charged again.

"Are you serious?" I said. "You're going to take this to an outside court, for having orange juice?"

He knew I had done nothing wrong, but he was pissed off and just wanted to get me somehow. I said, "I'll go to the papers. They love a story about harsh treatment."

"Give that back!" He snatched it from me then. I'd fucked him again.

He fucked me back the next day, though. They moved me. There was no winning in jail; they were always in control.

They told me I was going back to London, but typically, the authorities ended up sending me further north, up the motorway to Hatfield in Yorkshire. The good thing was that I got categorised D, meaning I was low risk now, and so I got put on a really nice wing. There were a couple of solicitors on the wing. One of them was doing nine years, and was getting towards the end of it. Another was doing six and a half.

I worked in the kitchen. There was a PO who wore a hat like Corporal Jones in *Dad's Army*. He made the most amazing Scotch eggs, although he was a proper bully. There was another woman called Mrs Smith. She used to take the convicts out and buy them fish and chips. She obviously became a legend in there. I was on the servery, dishing out the meals, and I met all the other inmates. That's how I met John Darwin, the canoe man who had faked his own death. He's a funny character, and I kind of looked after him in there. He was being bullied because they'd put him on the young offenders' wing for some reason. They were horrible to him. He had been a screw years before, and in jail that's a bad thing. Normally an ex-screw could not be in a normal location. If they broke the rules and ended up in nick, they were treated like sex offenders. John had got six years for his part in the fraud, all because of the media attention. If he hadn't been in the papers, it's unlikely that kind of fraud would have got him that long. That was why I'd been lucky to stay out of the spotlight. But now I was determined not to be any kind of criminal. It wasn't worth the stress and the pain that it put other people through.

CHAPTER THIRTY-SIX

The Road to Going Straight

Lynn made me suffer a bit before she finally came to visit me. I didn't blame her. I'd lied to her for years about being on the run. Lynn had had no idea. And why would I tell her? But eventually she came with the kids. I was so happy, I hadn't lost her.

Zack was 10 at the time. When he caught sight of me, he started crying.

"What's up with him?" I asked.

"He doesn't like that he has to see his dad in here! What the fuck is wrong with you?" she replied.

At that moment something changed inside me. *Look at what I've done,* I thought. *I've let them all down just by trying to give them something I never had. I thought the answer was money, but they don't need money, they need me. Now here I am in prison, pushing all of my trauma on to them.* Josh had never cried when he came to see me in Belmarsh. He was so young, and was just happy to see his dad. It would have just been a day out for him, with my nan, grandad and Lynn. So it had never prompted me to look at it from their perspective the first time round. I had been so busy feeling sorry for myself that it hadn't crossed my mind.

I knew then that I was done with committing crime, but without crime, how was I going to support them? Job prospects for ex-offenders are not great.

Salty and I had been to see *Catch Me If You Can* when it came out around 2003, and I had become fascinated by Frank Abagnale's story. Not only the criminality, but how he turned his life around at the end, after prison and became a fraud prevention expert. I felt a real affinity with Frank. There is one scene where he looks through the window at his mum with another man and his new sister. Anyone whose parent or parents left when they were a kid understands that scene more than most. That is what a normal life looks like to anyone who has not had one. Could I use my criminal experience to make money legitimately?

After Lynn's visit I went back to the wing and spoke to a guy called Dennis Eyre. I told him I wanted to go straight and I needed his help.

Dennis was an aristocrat serving time for money laundering. He was a big guy who loved his grub. Because I worked in the kitchens, I'd smuggle him lumps of cheese and half a loaf of bread from time to time. We'd all sit in his cell and play cards – me, Mark Sibbeck, Stretch and Gerry.

Dennis would be the banker. Here we all were, trusting the lord of fraud with our money – or Mars bars, in this case. He would take all the bets and distribute the

Mars bars to the winners. I was not actually a gambler, but in nick, I loved a bit of Mars bar gambling!

Dennis said to me, "If you want to go straight, I can get you into the Home Office. I know people in there."

"Okay. And…?" I replied, puzzled.

He said he could set up a meeting. But it was just jail talk. I just thought, *Yeah, whatever.*

CHAPTER THIRTY-SEVEN

Home Office

I came out of prison on 10 December 2010 knowing I would never go back. It was snowing. When you leave jail they give you about £70, so I went and bought some beers with another guy who was going back to London, Gerry. They gave me a travel warrant as well. I had a few beers with Gerry on the train, then I gave him a score to crack on from Elephant and Castle, and went back home.

I was put on tag, and that meant I had to be indoors from 7 pm to 7 am. That kind of ruled out taxi driving, because the best hours were gone. I could have got my hours changed, but I just wanted to reflect for a while. For the first month, I didn't talk to anybody, didn't even tell them I was out.

I had no debts outstanding, I had got rid of all the bad money. I now had a clean slate and was fresh to start over again, for the first time in years. We'd had an ex-council flat on an estate in Kent that we'd rented out; we stripped it and painted it all out like new.

I hadn't even spent a night in there before I got nicked. I was selling phones to Salty so I could buy new furniture for Lynn.

To an extent, our hero Frank Abagnale was a one-trick pony. After we saw the film, I went and read his book, one of the only ones I'd finished cover to cover. And what you learn about Abagnale, as much as I look up to the guy, is that he wasn't brought up criminally minded; he wasn't connected to other criminals or their networks. He hadn't even had another job, so he had nothing on his CV. When he came out of prison on parole in the 1970s, he was bagging groceries for a living. By contrast, I'd driven a cab, in shops, in my dad's printers, I'd had 4 kids, and I had stolen a fortune. *All of those experiences must be good for something?*

It took years for Abagnale to move from menial jobs into fraud prevention. He got his big break when he pitched a seminar on cheque fraud to a bank, and they went for it. So he went to work for the other side, and became an expert in fraud prevention.

For me, things moved more quickly. I'd met Dennis inside, who could get me into the Home Office straight away. I knew enough about prison life to know that as soon as he left those gates, I'd probably never hear from him again. He'd drift back into his own circles; everything he'd said in prison was just bullshit to get along.

So I was quite surprised when I was at home with Lynn and the phone rang.

"Hello, is that Tony?" I recognised the posh voice straight away.

"Dennis, good to hear from you, bruv! How's tricks, getting back to normal?" I asked.

"All good thanks, Tone. I'm calling to see if you're still interested in the Home Office," he replied.

Excited, I replied, "Interested? Damn right I am!"

"Let me make some calls and I'll get back to you," he promised, and hung up.

Dennis wasn't a bullshitter. Within three months of my release from jail, true to his word, Dennis called his man in Whitehall. He arranged for me to meet him and pitch my idea to use my criminal experience to help them combat fraud. Dennis came down and slept on my sofa the night before taking me there the next morning.

The Home Office is a huge, intimidating building just off Horseferry Road. I put a suit on, feeling quite nervous. What Dennis didn't know was that I'd made a fake passport in a moody name and took that in with me to use as my ID. To get into a government department you have to go through a few security checks, body scanners, and pods. Then you show the ID to the security staff at the counter. This passport fooled them all.

It was probably illegal, but so what? I wasn't doing it for crime anymore. I had a higher purpose now.

The meeting was with the head of fraud for the UK government, and from his attitude, I was glad I had done what I had done. I tossed the passport on his desk and told him, "I got through all your security with that. Your system's flawed. I'm two doors along from the Home Secretary. I could be anybody – a terrorist."

This top civil servant was absolutely fuming. He could barely speak. He just looked at the passport for about 10 minutes, and then he fobbed me off. He told me there was something called GAD – the Government's Actuary Department. They dealt with real documents, and they were the ones who could provide official passports. They did it for spies and undercover police officers, and maybe some high-level criminals who had moles inside the department. He said, "I'd only be interested if it was GAD," meaning he'd only be interested if I had somehow managed to obtain an official passport via bribery or some other method. Never mind that the government had passed my moody one off as genuine on my way in here.

They knew that biometric passports – which hold identifying information on a chip in the passport – had just been rolled out that same year, 2010, and that would make it almost impossible to counterfeit. It would require a lot more legwork to generate a British biometric passport.

And anyway, that missed the point that most of the time, passports weren't looked at as carefully as they were at a border. You could still do a lot of damage with a passport that just looked the part.

I did not get the chance to tell him that his biometric passports wouldn't deter serious criminals. He wasn't interested in what I had to say. I went home dispirited, but not defeated. There had to be a way for me to use my knowledge to help people. No one knew who I was. I had to find a way to get myself out there.

CHAPTER THIRTY-EIGHT

A New Man

I went to see one of my other mates, Paddy, who was a street fixer for journalists. A company I'd never heard of called Vice were filming a documentary about dangerous dogs in East London. I went to see him on location, and they seemed to keep following me. *Take the camera off me!*

But after Paddy finished at the end of the day, he said, "The film crew are interested in you. They clocked that you've got an electronic tag on your ankle. I think you should meet these guys from Vice."

So, I went to meet Will Fairman, series director, who said they were interested in doing a documentary on fraud. Paddy had told him I was the dog's bollocks at it in my criminal days. To begin with, I thought it was all a bit Mickey Mouse: in 2011, YouTube wasn't what it is today, and internet videos weren't yet as popular or influential as TV.

The series producer was a tabloid journalist and author called Graham Johnson. He'd just branched out into doing edgy stuff for Vice, but he mainly worked as a crime reporter. At one point he had worked for the *Sun*, and he was also the Investigations Editor for the *Sunday Mirror*. Vice were exploring crime too, but for a younger, cooler audience.

Most TV people come from a middle-class background, and they find crime fascinating. But it can be hard for different backgrounds to understand each other. I wanted to get myself out there to show people why criminals committed crime.

"What can you show us?" they asked me. "We want to see some old-school fraud."

"Have you ever heard of black money?" I said.

"We've heard of it, but never seen it," they replied.

Without a second thought, I made them an offer. "I can show you some of that, if you like?"

Their faces lit up. I took them to film black money with the 419 crew, my friends the Nigerian guys. That was the first time it had ever been broadcast – guys with their suitcases full of fake cash, all in masks. I was talking to the camera naturally, and the director liked how I came across. They were smart, though. They didn't offer me any money, even though I was now presenting that show. TV has strict rules about criminals getting paid.

I took them to see Sinner. They filmed us having pie and mash in Eltham, and I took them back to our gaff. I showed them a bunch of fake IDs. I was in my vest, looking like a bit of a wally, and they cut it to urban music. I gave them what they wanted, taking them into shops and showing them how easy it was to blag a phone on strap. They lapped it up. Then they said they wanted a big house scene. So Graham said, "Why don't you ask Dave Courtney?"

Although Dave was with Jenny Pinto, the girl who gave me my first pair of skates, I had always stayed far from the limelight. Dave, of course, had been in the limelight. I had always preferred the shadows. I had always said hello to him and nodded my head in respect, but I never interacted criminally with him. I reached out to Jen, and she told me to come round. When I arrived at Camelot Castle (Dave's house), Jenny welcomed me with a big cuddle. "Come in, T, Dave's in there," she told me, pointing to the front room.

I walked into a room covered with guns and knives all over the walls. On top of that there were pictures of every gangster from yesteryear. I sat and chatted with Dave for ages. He was a pioneer for many of the old-school lot from the underworld. His friendship with Freddie Foreman is still as strong as ever because of it. He was the one that got most of these old-school guys to speak and share their stories. I told him what the show was about, and why I was doing it. He said we could use his place, and he would love to be in it. A few days later we were at his place to film.

After the filming was all over, Dave gave me a pep talk. "People will call you a grass, Tony. People will be jealous. Even people that you think are your friends will turn against you."

This was long before the documentary came out. Dave had been through all those things.

The Vice documentary, *How To Get Away With Stealing*, has 11.5 million views at the time of writing. In 2011 they screened it at the Sundance Film Festival in a cinema in Leicester Square, and it's still available on YouTube. I did a Q&A onstage afterwards. That was my first experience of public speaking. There was plenty that didn't get shown in the final version, but it was all good fun.

I got along well with Graham, who had done a lot of legwork, understood the underworld, and had written books about big cartels, including infamous debt collectors like Stephen French, who had worked with Big Man, targeting other criminals.

I was really useful to Graham. I got him and Vice into loads of places, so they started paying me as a fixer. One item was about bare-knuckle boxing: I had told them about the bouts I had seen in Dave Courtney's back garden. The video got millions of views. That never would have happened if I hadn't introduced them to Dave, who hosted the fights.

When the 2011 riots happened, I kept Sky News and the others up to date on the front line, getting them access to people who had been involved in the riots. There was a music group who won an award with a track that sampled an interview I'd supplied Sky with. Because I knew so many people on the front line, they wanted to talk about their issues. It was the first time they'd truly been able to put their point across. Those people who were rioting had a voice, and they wanted to talk, because they felt oppressed, as if no-one was listening. Looting and burning stores are not the actions of people without issues. To understand them, we have to understand the problem.

I was using my connections, but I was out of the life of crime forever. I had no regrets, and I was happy. Money had never made me happy. But having a job, working for myself, and realising I was good at something other than crime – it made me feel good.

There were still times when I was tested. I bumped into a friend of a friend, who I had done a few moves with back when I was at it. He had served time for robbery, and was known as a big player, still very much active when he caught sight of me at a party.

He said, "T, long time bro. I got something I wanna chat to you about. Shall we go for a smoke?"

We went up to the rooftop, looking out at the London skyscrapers, the ones I'd seen going up since I was a kid in Greenwich. It was like film scenery: the city I had lived in, lost myself in, brought children into, and stolen from. Now, when I thought I'd finally found myself, here was this guy, suddenly telling me he'd got a move for £2 million. Not a stunt for the cameras – a bank transfer involving taking over somebody's account.

I stopped him in mid-flow. "Bruv, I'm out. It was never about the money for me. I have a life now. Bro, you should go find yourself, find out who you are."

He looked at me like I was a nutcase. I guess, to him, I am. He still thought money was going to make him happy – and it will for a minute, but minutes go quickly.

During the riots, Graham came to me with a different proposition. Now that looting was a big story, he wanted me to set up cameras in a house on an estate in south east London to film a car they'd parked there as bait, and wait for it to be vandalised.

It wasn't for me, this one. I turned it down. So instead of using me, the guy with the cameras cut a side deal with the resident of a flat. When he came back to inspect the footage, the resident said he'd had some mates over, and they'd stolen the cameras!

I knew how some people in the media can use you, and I'd always made it clear to Graham that I would never connect him with anyone for him to turn them over. Big stories always have some guy turned over. If a journalist was looking to nail somebody, I'd say no. I couldn't get involved with that. It was as good as grassing. Perhaps I was breaking the *omertà* code with the work I was doing now, but I certainly never grassed on anyone. I had never done so when I was a criminal either.

CHAPTER THIRTY-NINE

Retail Risk

Since my release from prison in 2010, I had appeared on the BBC, Vice, CNN and Channel 5, to name a few. In 2012, with acclaimed documentaries on my CV, I took all my TV footage and edited it together myself, using basic software. I sent it to a company called Retail Risk, applying to be one of their speakers. I'd applied the previous year but been knocked back – they said they'd already got a fraudster talking, and didn't need another one. At the time, I thought, *Fuck, just my luck! I go straight and so does some other guy*.

I chanced my luck again, sending over my "show reel" that I had crudely cobbled together, and within 20 minutes Retail Risk call me saying they'd got a spot for me if I wanted to speak at their event in London in three weeks' time. I spent the next three weeks building my presentation.

When the day came, my turn to speak was at 3 pm. I sat there nervously, waiting for the woman before me to finish. I got up there and told them some bits about what I knew. I had put images up to accompany my speech, and was just talking away. The all had very serious faces, and the room was silent. All the while, I was thinking to myself, *Nope, they don't like me.* I came to the end of the presentation and they all just sat there, looking stunned. Then they all clapped, and as I walked off stage, I was mobbed. I stood answering questions from all these guys working at huge brands for two whole hours. What I didn't know was that in the background Mark Emmott, a successful marketing guy and partner in Retail Risk, was watching me.

I got home that night and checked my emails. I had an email from a speaker bureau in the US that had an enquiry about me. They wanted to know if I had a show reel I could send over. I called the conference owner Paul Beasant, thanked him for letting me speak, and asked him for the footage of my talk. He had missed it but told me that the feedback for the event had been great. His business partner watched it, and wanted to take me to lunch.

I met Paul in Browns restaurant. I told him that companies get it wrong: the people are always the vulnerability. It is all about testing and training.

He said he thought that he could win some business for me, and said he would like us to go into business together. He would bring in his partner Mark, and we could create something together.

The idea was that I would get paid by big companies to go and find their security weaknesses. Basically, I'd do what I'd been doing as a criminal, without stealing anything, and then report back to them on what I'd found.

Mark watched my presentation closely and said it was rubbish – not structured enough. But he liked the Q&A: "That's where you thrive," he said. "You're great when you're talking with people."

We did something really simple: we got a suite upstairs in the hotel at the next conference they did. They had a database for all the loss-prevention specialists who came to their events. The *Sun* newspaper had written an article about me and called me "Britain's Greatest Fraudster", so Mark emailed his clients, asking if they wanted to come and meet Tony Sales, using Britain's Greatest Fraudster as a tag line to put bums on seats. All these people worked for the same companies I'd been robbing as a criminal. Argos, Currys, and the rest. We filled up 10 appointments in no time. Three big names signed up to take our test. We would hit all three in the way only we could. Loss prevention teams were always testing their own systems: they wanted to know their vulnerabilities. They knew loads, but finding the holes they hadn't yet identified was the key.

Most of these clients I can't discuss for obvious reasons, but one of the people we spoke to was the head of loss for B&Q, Ray Palmer. He was a well-respected guy in the loss prevention world. Ray knows his onions.

In B&Q the staff wear orange aprons, and I had been into the Greenwich branch before we met and nicked one. When Ray came into the hotel suite for our meeting, he saw the B&Q apron hanging up on the coat stand. He told me later that that was what sold him. He knew straight away what I could do with that apron alone. I could pose as staff, go in the backroom and mingle in the staff areas. The apron was the key to accessing behind the scenes. If I had wanted to, I could have just put the apron on and walk into restricted areas of the store, taking what I wanted.

What I didn't know was that B&Q had had a similar problem, losing a small fortune to a shoplifting gang. I discovered how they were getting hit, and showed Ray how to fix their security problems.

For one company, I broke their refund system. After I had done it, I went to their head office to show them how. I had managed to steal something from the store, take it in and get a refund.

As I showed them in the meeting, one of the company's employees said, "There is no way you have broken that system!"

What I didn't know at the time was that it had cost them several million quid to implement that system across their estate. I had just walked in and broken it in three days. *Oops!* To add insult to injury, I put the money from the refunded stolen goods into money bags and put them on the table during the meeting. The impact was huge, and it solidified our corporate friendship. They showed faith in me, and I didn't let them down.

For the next 18 months I was all over the place. Paul and Mark were building their empire and I was enjoying seeing some of the world. My career was building and life was ticking over smoothly. Most importantly for me, Nan and Grandad were really proud of what I was doing.

CHAPTER FORTY

Nan

It was coming to the end of 2013, and my nan had been ill for a while. She had heart problems and had had a defibrillator fitted. "I hate this fucking thing, son," she used to tell me all the time.

In 2005, good John had gone into a travel agent and asked them to suggest somewhere that was warm for a holiday.

The travel agent said, "How about the Gambia?"

"Alright," John said, "I'll give it a try!"

There was a bloke in the Croydon branch of the travel agent who was from there. He told John he'd have a good time there.

John went and told Nan, and next thing they were off. "I hope it's not like Kenya," Nan said, "because I fucking hated it there."

But Nan loved it. "They were so good to us," John told me. "They had a hotel and a bar on the beach called Solomon's, and they treated us like royalty. For Nan, it almost felt like a second home." Nan went back to the Gambia every year after that.

By January 2014, she knew she was dying. But she'd got it into her head that we should all go for one last trip. "They have good heart doctors in Gambia," she said, "so if anything does go wrong, I'll be alright."

I don't know where she got that idea. I knew that the health system there wouldn't be as good as it is in the UK. But once my nan was convinced of something, she wouldn't change her mind. I begged her not to go, and Lynn went over to see her and begged her not to go too.

But she was having none of it. "If I die out there, I die, at least I'll be in a beautiful place." And that settled it. Nan, Grandad, Mum, John, Kate, and my nephew TJ decided to fly out on 3 January 2014. I couldn't go, as I had business to attend to at home.

They had been out there for a few days when I got a call to say Nan was ill. I was in the gym when my phone rang. Nan was getting incubated and put in an induced coma. When they incubated her, Mum and Kate stood at the end of the bed, watching. It should have taken seconds, my mum said, but they were at it for hours, putting the tube in, pulling it out. There was blood everywhere.

Nan was still unconscious, on life support. The hotel people were so nice to the rest of the family – they said they could stay free of charge for as long as they wanted, until Nan was all sorted out. But their visas ran out, so they had to return home and leave my nan out there in a Gambian hospital, with my grandad by her side. Their love to the end was beautiful.

Shortly afterwards, Nan was airlifted over the border to Senegal, where they said she would get proper treatment, and I went out to see her. I've been to some places in the world, but I'd never seen anything like Senegal. There were hundreds of people lined up in a gauntlet, begging to take me for a ride as I came out of the airport. Heathrow and Gatwick were nothing by comparison. I bundled into a cab. The insurance company had given my grandad a chaperone, and he came to meet me at the airport.

I got to the car, and my grandad was sitting inside, waiting for me. He looked tired but pleased to see me. I told the driver I wanted to go straight to the hospital. I wanted to see my nan.

When I finally walked in there, after 10 hours of travelling, it wasn't a hospital ward – just a room with a hospital bed in it, and a woman sitting there.

"What are you doing here?" I asked.

"Looking after her," she said.

"Would you give us a minute, please?" I asked her.

I saw my nan there in the hospital bed. She was unconscious and there was barely a breeze in this hot room. She was hooked up to a heart monitor, with wires and tubes all over her. At that point I knew. I touched her hand and held it. As I did, I saw her heart rate increase on the monitor. She knew I was there. She had waited for me to arrive. I told her, "It's ok, Nan, I am here now. I will make sure everything is ok, just like always."

After the hospital, I went back to the hotel and went to bed. I wanted to be up and at the hospital in the morning, to try and get her moved home. I pulled the sheets over myself and crashed out.

At 1:50 am, I sat bolt upright, gasping for breath. I couldn't breathe. I took a drink of water and lay back down. Just as I was nodding off again, the phone rang. It was the chaperone.

Nan had passed away 10 minutes before. I had felt it.

Calling my grandad and breaking the news to him was the hardest thing I have ever had to do. Telling someone so beautiful that his queen had left was heartbreaking. The memory of it still brings me to tears. My nan was the first person I had lost who I truly loved. She was the one person who had always been there for me right from the start. She never did things by halves.

I visited a funeral parlour to find that the morticians had even embalmed her wrong. All her skin was falling off. They claimed they couldn't tell us the cause of death due to the Official Secrets Act. Grandad, Mum and John were fuming about it. "She wasn't James Bond!"

Finally, we were able to come home and say goodbye to Nan. The crematorium was packed. Nan had always wanted to be cremated. "Don't put me in the ground with those fucking worms," she would say. The only thing I ever saw her scared of snakes and worms.

She had a great send off. All her friends came to say goodbye. It was a sad day, but she would have been proud. We had the wake at the Surdoc Club in Bermondsey.

My nan's death made me focus on my work much more. Now more than ever, I really wanted to make her proud.

CHAPTER FORTY-ONE

The Passport

Since working with Retail Risk I had been getting bookings as a public speaker and a lot more TV appearances. Although I was always very protective of the people I put in front of the cameras, I was less careful when it came to my own reputation.

Paul Connolly, an Irish investigative reporter for Channel 5, came to me for a show called *Black Market Britain: Undercover Sting*. I said I'd never stitch somebody up, but I ended up screwing myself over.

We started off renting cars in fake names. I went into a hire place and pulled a car out as Paul, using his driving licence and card. It was filmed undercover and went out on TV.

Then Paul came back to me for a story about passports. I had a passport in my old name, the one I'd used on the run, and changed the photo for his. He was going to try and cross from Dover to Calais with it, to see if he could get past border control with somebody else's documents. Biometrics weren't an issue, because this was an old passport from before 2011, so it didn't need any of that info. It was just a straight photo swap.

Connolly seemed nervous as he approached passport control. But next thing you know, the camera cut to him on the other side, sipping a glass of wine. "Hello, I'm here in France! I got through, I can't believe it." *Fucking hell*, I thought, *I can't believe it still worked!*

Then he came back, but he said in the show that he got arrested. They didn't charge him. He told them there was a legitimate purpose – public interest – and they let him go.

But there were consequences for me. About six months later I went to Madrid, to give a talk at a conference for a security company. Giving speeches was becoming part of my everyday life, travelling the world to share the stage with some of the world's biggest names, including ex-footballers, jockeys, and TV show hosts.

I checked into the hotel in Madrid and was smoking out the window. There's a ritual I go through in pressurised situations – heists in the past, and now public speeches – every time I make an appearance, I will have my Beats on and Dr Dre playing to get me into the zone. I finished my cigarette, and went downstairs to scout out the venue. I had a look around, because I wanted to know everything about the environment. As I went through the lobby, two coppers were speaking with the hotel manager. "Mr Sales!" he called. "There are two policemen here to see you."

Blimey. I'd only checked in an hour ago.

"Do you have your passport?"

"Yes, thanks."

"Let us see it, please."

I gave it to them.

"Thank you. Sorry to disturb." And they left.

What the fuck was that all about?

I did the talk; the audience was brilliant, and I really enjoyed it. I headed back to the airport, but at passport control, something flagged on the system. The immigration cops took away the passport, had a natter in Spanish, returned it to me, and I was allowed on the plane. I thought nothing of it – because I'd obviously got a reputation, so it was to be expected.

Not long after, I got booked for a talk in Vienna. And it was the same deal again. I got into Austria without any problems, but as I was on the way back, I got to the gates and I could see this blonde lady's face change.

"Is anything the matter?" I asked.

"Yes, you have a warning against your passport," she said.

"What for?" I ask.

"You need to contact the Paris Police."

They took me into a room and questioned me, conferring with border control. I told them it was because I'd made a passport for TV. *Can you add it to the system, or get it taken off?* It was also stopping me from going to France at all. I'd been told that if I went there, I'd get nicked.

The Austrian cops were really nice. One of them even recognised me, and that gave me a little buzz. He said he would see what he could do. He made a note of it on the system, but said I'd most likely have to speak to the Paris Police.

When I got back, that is what I did. I rang them, but unsurprisingly, it was all in French. *Fuck that, my English is bad enough.*

I told several border forces why I made that passport: it was to improve their security. But the only way I can clear it is during an official review every three years by the French authorities. It's had two reviews already and been declined. The show was seven years ago at the time of writing, and the same procedure now happens to me every time I leave the country. I get taken out of line and questioned, and it can take hours while they go through all the checks and reviews. That is the price I will always have to pay. But it's not such a bad outcome, all things considered.

Mark called me up one day and told me that he has been approached by some TV guy who wanted me to be in his new drama that they were pitching to Channel 4, called *Crooks*. "Right up your street," he said.

Adam Boome was developing a TV drama which examined the real reasons and ways people committed crime. The idea was that it would be written with former criminals working with TV writers, and also acted by them.

We hit it off, and within a few weeks I had become the main character in the drama. Then we also began developing a documentary following the work I was doing with Retail Risk, breaking into businesses and reporting what I found. It would make for great TV.

Channel 4 were interested, and JD Sports were up for being in the pilot episode. Channel 4 wanted me to steal a million pounds' worth of stock. They would call the show *Heist* (in the days before Sky's show of the same name).

CHAPTER FORTY-TWO

The Boxer & Nearly Losing Everything

My star was rising. I was getting all this positive attention for the first time in my life. I went to see a friend at his shop. The door went, and it was Anthony Small, the professional boxer. He was a kid from Deptford who at one time was the Intercontinental Champion in the light middleweight division. We'd become mates, and I went to lots of his fights when I was younger and still criminally active. His entrance music was always "Superbad" by James Brown, and he came out on a skateboard, wearing a Scream mask.

One night I went to see him fight Bradley Pryce at the O2 Arena, on the Amir Khan undercard. It was a wicked night. Willy Lamond put Khan on his arse in the first round, and Amir stormed back to win. Lynn and I were sitting ringside, because Anthony had got us in. Just before Anthony's entrance, instead of the usual James Brown song, a Muslim prayer came on.

"Who's this?" I wondered. "Is this Bradley Pryce?"

No, it was him.

The year was 2004 – a time of racial and religious division, particularly after the 9/11 terrorist attacks, which were still very present in people's minds. I wasn't sure why he had brought religion into the boxing ring. I knew Anthony liked to be a bit controversial, but I was confused. He lost that fight – the ref stepped in in the seventh round – and soon his life would head in a different direction.

Not long after, he was on the front page of the *Sun*, burning a poppy. My grandparents lived through the war. When that story came out, I decided to cut ties with him. He was an intelligent man, but I felt he was going off in a different direction.

I hadn't seen him for more than six years when he put his head round the door. My first words to him were, "You burnt the poppy, bro. What the fuck?"

He went straight into a long rant about the corruption of the poppy campaign, British imperialism and the American government. I said it was about the feelings of families, and it was important to the generations of today. Did he realise how much my grandparents suffered after the war?

When he knew he was getting nowhere with me, he said, "Look, I got a problem. I need you to help me."

"Mate, I don't do anything in that world anymore. I'm out," I replied.

"Bruv, come and meet me next week. Let's talk, please. I really need your help," he said.

I really didn't want to go and meet him, but started ringing me, nagging, blowing up my phone, and so finally I gave in. "Alright, where shall I meet you?"

We arranged to meet in Lidl car park on Southend Lane. When I arrived, sitting in the car opposite were two people in a Land Rover who looked like Old Bill. Anthony came along and got in the car. "Yo, what's happening, bruv?"

"There's Old Bill watching us," I said.

"You're paranoid!"

"Maybe. Let's get out of here." So we drove away. I pulled a few manoeuvres and turn around in the middle of the road. What was coming the other way? The Land Rover, with the two spooks looking shocked. Anthony was proper hot, I could feel it.

"They are on you, bro," I told him.

"No, don't be silly. No one's on me."

I ditched the car in a back road, and we went to a cafe and sat outside. We were just making general conversation because I didn't want any heat. Then the Land Rover appeared again, slowed down and did a three-point turn right in front of us, as though they were taking pictures.

"Bruv, you're proper hot," I said. "They're Old Bill, and I feel really uncomfortable. Whatever you want to talk about, let's put the phones in the cars and talk like that."

Because they'd already got a picture of me meeting him, there was no point walking away. I was curious about what he had to say. So, as we left the cafe, I covered my mouth as we talked, so there couldn't be any lip-reading.

I told him I was out of that world, and I didn't want it to jeopardise my life and new career. It wouldn't be fair on me.

Anthony called me again and again. He was so persistent. But I told him, in no uncertain terms, "I can't get passports anymore."

I hadn't even tried, but I didn't have to tell him that. I didn't want anything to do with this.

CHAPTER FORTY-THREE

No Knock this Time

BOOM! At 4 am, my door was broken down. Armed police stormed in, pointing lasers at us. They snatched my missus and kids. All in separate rooms.

I kicked off. "Who the fuck are you, coming into my house? Have you seen my record? I'm not having that…"

I wanted to defend my family. This was primal instinct taking over.

"We ain't normal police, Tony. Sit down," they said.

"What do you mean, you ain't normal police? You got wings or something? Who are you, the Power Rangers?" I snapped back.

"Why are we here, Tony?" he asked.

"What sort of question's that?! How am I supposed to know why the fuck you're in my house? You tell me. I'd really like to know!" I was wound up now, adrenaline pumping.

Then he pulled out a ring binder. They had scans of Anthony's picture on all different passports. Portuguese, Spanish, French. "That's why we're here."

This cunt. I started to calm down. I knew I'd done nothing wrong.

The police must have known I hadn't supplied him with those passports, because they'd been listening to all the calls. We'd been under observation the whole time. The cops had followed me in Dubai and shadowed me out there. I hadn't clocked them, because I wasn't doing anything wrong – and even if I had, you're unlikely to notice spooks at that level.

True, the fact that I had clocked them the first time in the Land Rover had made me behave in a suspicious manner. So my vigilance, my awareness of criminality, was now coming back to haunt me in new, weird ways.

"You'd better level with us," the copper said, "else you're going to be involved with all this, and you don't know what it is."

"No comment," I replied.

They arrested me and took me down to the station. They kicked Lynn and kids out of their own home, without giving them anywhere to go or stay – they just told them to get out. They spent two days ransacking and bugging my house.

I was held at Borough Police Station, and I had no idea what was coming. It was a different kind of cell, with a TV screen embedded in the wall showing David Attenborough nature documentaries on repeat. They reckoned that calmed people down.

I was kicking back in the cell, trying to relax, when there was a knock on the door. "It's prayer time."

"What do you mean?" I was puzzled.

"Do you want to go to the prayer room?" they asked.

"I'm an atheist, I don't believe in god," I replied.

"Okay." A few hours later: "It's tea time. Halal food?"

"No, I'm *not* religious. I'll eat anything." I started to realise what was going on.

They come back with a halal chicken burger and chips, and a can of drink. I ate it while watching David Attenborough, and went to sleep.

Next morning: "Halal breakfast?"

"Nah mate, I want a *full English*. I want bacon, sausage, eggs and tomatoes." I was going to enjoy this.

Later, they took me to the interview room.

"There's a light on the ceiling that's red," I was told. "If at any time it goes green, that means somebody else from somewhere else is watching."

"What do you mean, somebody else, somewhere else?"

"Let your imagination run wild."

"Anthony Small..." the copper began. He pulled several A4 copies of passports out and put them on the table, and the green light went on. Whoever was behind the light was now listening in. "We know Mr Small asked you to make him a passport. All we want to know is, where is it?"

"There isn't one," I responded.

Even though I had a lawyer, I wasn't getting legal aid. It was all coming out of my own pocket. This was the price I would always pay for my past.

I was out for good. I was never going to make a passport for anybody again. We were pitching *Heist* to Channel 4, and they were up for it. My talks and other work with Retail Risk were going well, and I was happy in my new life. Now, suddenly, everything was up in the air.

The Old Bill took me back to my cell, before hauling me back to the interview room once more. This time the light didn't go on. I said "No comment" to everything. And they let me out. But when I got out, the story was in the newspapers.

According to the papers, a white British guy called Simon Keeler, who called himself Sulayman Keeler, had gone to Russia to buy a plane, to fill it with AK47s before flying out to Syria. They were going over there to distribute them.

The police had released me on bail, pending further enquiries. Anthony went to court and was found not guilty. The jury cleared him of all charges.

The CPS had no evidence linking me to terrorism, because there was none. But they still suspected me of something. So they put me on the hook for whatever they could, to use as leverage. They decided to charge me for possession of a fraudulent implement and counterfeit money.

During their enquiries, they'd found a fraudulent documents warehouse somewhere in North London that had supplied Anthony with his passports, and they thought I was part of it. But I wasn't. I had nothing to do with it.

When they raided my home, all they could find was a fake driving licence and a counterfeit 50 euro note. They'd found it on the bedside table – it wasn't hidden.

These were things I used in my new fraud prevention career to demonstrate to clients.

The fake 50 euro note was only printed on one side. It was printed really well – I had it to show onstage at conferences. It was a stage prop. Because it was blank on the other side, there was no chance I would have been able to use it.

The trouble was that I didn't have official permission to have fake notes or driving licences. And the cop who arrested me was new to the terrorist squad; he probably wanted to notch up a few prosecutions. But I would never in my life have had anything to do with something as low as that.

I was gutted, because I could still be tainted with it. My reputation in crime prevention would be ruined if I was shown to be still actively involved with crime. No reputable company would want to work with me.

They charged me with possession of a fraudulent implement and counterfeit money. The money carried a sentence of up to 15 months in jail, and the driving licence 12 months. I could be looking at two and a half years in prison.

Despite all the evidence I had showing legitimate reasons for having those items, I had to go to court to clear my name. It was the first time I had ever pleaded not guilty. The first time I would face a trial with a jury, barristers, and cross-examination. I was absolutely fuming, because I could go to jail for longer than when I got caught red-handed and went on the run for six years. And I had to pay for my own defence.

I faced the charges of possessing the driving licence and notes at Southwark Crown Court. They'd raided me on suspicion of terrorism, but this case no longer had anything to do with that. The CPS had one of the top prosecutors trying to nail me. Not because they thought I was guilty of using the licence or the note – that was clearly nonsense. The arresting officer thought I was something to do with the terror plot – but he wasn't allowed to say it explicitly.

It was extraordinarily stressful because I had so much riding on it. My defence was that I had them for work, for research. My barrister said there was a good chance the jury would understand it and clear me.

The trouble was, I'd been a criminal, so many automatically assumed I must be bad. I had this my whole life: even when I went onstage to speak, when I was standing around people, they'd joke, "Put your wallets away!" I'd take it in good humour, and I had to accept that I'd be tarred with that brush for the rest of my life. But words got lost. I couldn't let those assumptions become reality.

Mark and Adam came to my trials and testified that I was now a legitimate fraud consultant. Adam took the stand and showed them videos of my TV appearances, explaining how I had changed my life, and how my intentions were now to *prevent* fraud. I nearly cried when I saw it onscreen. Here I was, having to justify my new life all because Anthony was too selfish to care about the effect his actions had on others.

I had to be cross-examined by their barrister. It made me nervous, but I was also confident, because for the first time, I knew I didn't have to lie. I could tell the truth, because I had done nothing wrong.

While telling my story about how I got in to fraud prevention, I mentioned what I had done at the Home Office. As soon as I mentioned the HO head of fraud by name, a member of the jury started writing a note. Then she got the judge's attention and passed him the note.

"Er, we going to have to take a moment," the judge said. "Mr Sales, can you wait outside, please?"

So out I went. We were out there for about half an hour, before my brief came out. "Tony, listen. A member of the jury works at the home office, and she knows the head of fraud."

She was worried that might jeopardise the case, but the judge and prosecution were ok with it. They knew it would cost a fortune if we had to start the trial again.

Every question they asked I just batted back to them. They were trying to insinuate that there was a criminal motive for me having this stuff, because I'd previously been caught in possession of fake IDs with a criminal purpose. It was so obviously bullshit. It was a clear-cut case, because I had a reason to have those implements. I was a fraud prevention specialist, and I needed to understand the market.

However, I could see why they acted in the way they did, though, and in a sense it was reassuring that, after seeing someone with a record like mine meeting someone who was potentially going to commit an act of terror, the police and special agencies were on it so quickly.

It was a nervous moment waiting for the verdict. If I was found guilty I would never be able to work in fraud prevention again and probably not appear on TV again, not to mention going to prison.

I didn't have to worry for long, the verdict was came back in 45 minutes and I was cleared. When the trial was over, we came out of court, and I stood there, elated.

The jury came out, and one of them said to me, "We all knew you were innocent."

Then, as I was standing there, taking in the fact that I still had my freedom, Adam called.

"You'll never guess what. Channel 4 have commissioned your new series."

That's what I call a release.

CHAPTER FORTY-FOUR

Underworld TV

In 2016, the Brexit vote happened. On the day of the result, JD Sports decided they didn't want to give us an access agreement for the Channel 4 show. They couldn't risk bad PR after their share price had taken a kicking. If I was going to steal a million quid off them on telly, their shareholders might get offended. It was very disappointing.

Around that time my relationship with Retail Risk came to an end as well. We all shook hands and wished each other luck.

I had to do some hard thinking about the next step. By that time Adam and I were enjoying working together so much that we decided to go all in and form a TV production company together. The idea was to specialise in TV and film projects that furthered the understanding of the real causes of crime.

Crime is the most popular genre of fiction and documentaries about crime are all over TV, but 99% of them are made by nice middle-class people who have never done anything worse than speeding. We wanted people who had been on the other side to be creatively involved in telling their own stories.

We called our new company Underworld TV. We quickly found that there are lots of ex-offenders looking for a way into the creative industries. They've got talent and stories to tell but it's hard to break into the media when you come from a difficult background. Ex-offenders get offered jobs on building sites or in shoe repair shops but businesses don't generally think of them as intelligent, creative people with something to offer. That talent pool is a resource we are wasting as a society. Our first commission as UWTV was for Real Stories, a huge YouTube channel that shows human engaging stories, just like we wanted to make.

It was a documentary called it *Sorry I Shot You*. It was about a guy called Dean Stanna. His cousin Nicole Stanberry, another ex-offender, directed it and I produced it. It raised eyebrows in the underworld, because Dean wanted to say sorry to the copper that he shot. Without making excuses for Dean, Nicole told the story of how he had lost both parents before the age of 11 and how life had taken him down a criminal road. His brother and sisters appeared in the film and tried to figure out why he had become a criminal and they hadn't. Dean's story is so powerful, and I was so privileged to have been a part of it. I truly believe that it could only have been made by a team with first hand knowledge of the underworld.

I was getting everything sorted for the documentary launch party that we were having in Bermondsey, when my sister called me to tell me that Grandad had been taken into hospital. His breathing was really bad. I left and made my way to hospital to see him. He looked really tired; he had never really been the same after Nan died. It broke him. He was so strong his whole life, and to see him there looking so frail was devastating. We all went to see him for a final goodbye. We had a good chat, and I told him he was the most amazing dad I could have wished for. He was 83 when he died, and I still miss him.

That night I had to get up on stage in front of about 100 people and hold it all together, while the whole audience, including Dean's family was in tears at Dean's story. That was the hardest thing I had had to do. A couple of weeks later when we cremated him, I couldn't hold it in. I got up to give a speech and just crumbled. Charles Willis, one of Nan and Grandad's closest friends, took over. Then at the end when the casket was going in, they all started singing. It was beautiful. They will always live on with me and they are always with me, in my memories.

Sorry I Shot You was a success, and things were staring to hot up for me again. Our second commission was a series for Channel 4 called *What Makes A Murderer*. It was a dream project. We made it together with Dragonfly TV, and I found myself working in a big office for the first time ever. We persuaded three people who had committed murder to undergo physical and psychological tests on camera. They told their life stories, and two world experts, Professor Adrian Raine and Dr Vicky Thakordas-Desai, put the pieces together. We wanted to discover what had taken them from birth to the moment they committed murder, in order to understand how others could be prevented from taking that same path.

During the months of research and filming, I came to understand a lot more about my own journey. I was able to ask several forensic psychologists, who had dealt with thousands of violent criminals, how many they had met who had experienced significant trauma in childhood. They all agreed that there were virtually no exceptions to violent offenders having childhood trauma in their background.

TV needs to see the realities of the underworld without the preconceptions of what crime is. I have to try to make a difference, even if it only helps one kid or stops one shooting, one stabbing. My connections from the old days give me access to people who want to tell their stories, though they know they will mostly get demonised in the media. But we tried to show depth with our content, and explain why people had fallen into that world. You don't just become a criminal.

CHAPTER FORTY-FIVE

Andy

In a strange twist of fate, I met Andy at a fraud prevention conference. He is the former head of the Metropolitan Police fraud squad at New Scotland Yard. We had a lot of fascinating conversations, where we tried to figure out if we'd ever crossed paths, and why my crew got away with the vast majority of our crimes.

Andy was the referee on Channel 4's hit series *Hunted*, where members of the public had to go on the run and evade "law enforcement". He had also been the head of Special Investigations at SO15 Counter-Terrorism Command – retired before that fiasco I'd got muddled up with – and so he had to be careful about any association between us. He knew his friends from the Old Bill would give him heat about hanging around with someone who had high-security alerts against their passports. From their perspective, I'd been on TV, getting a bit of a name for myself. Was I just another celebrity criminal still dipping my toes in the criminal waters? They had to believe a guy like me, a master conman, wasn't pulling the wool over their eyes when I said I wanted to help people now.

If I could use what I'd learned to prevent crime, I was going to do it. People like me were needed, I told Andy, because I was the only person amongst all these corporations who had the keys to everybody's personal data, who truly knew how vulnerable we all are. After all, I stole data as a kid – I understand what can be done with just one single piece of the correct data.

Andy knew I wasn't bullshitting, and we were on the way to becoming business partners. Who'd have thought it: the cat and the mouse teaming up together!

CHAPTER FORTY-SIX

Solomon

In 2018 I met a computer whizz kid, Solomon Gilbert. This special 22-year-old got to know me by breaking into my hotel room after the CIFAS conference we both spoke at in Manchester. He'd cracked the door codes on my room, just like I used to do with the grabbers back in the day – but he was taking it from analogue to digital. A kid after my own heart! The first hacker I had met in the eight years I had been straight who was worthy.

What is a hack? Why does it happen? There's nearly always a criminal endgame. But Solomon was rare, because for him, it was all about the puzzle. Like when Neo is looking at the screen in *The Matrix*, and everyone else can only see numbers, but he sees the picture. I've met hackers and crackers; I've tested them all. I give them a test, and none of them have broken it except Solomon.

While he was still a schoolkid Bristol, he'd downed the American Nazi party website. He got in, took over, and got access to all their membership information. I was almightily impressed. Not long after, the school found a USB stick and they kicked him out. The Old Bill came and took the stick, and he asked them if they wanted the password. "No," they said, "we don't need it."

The Old Bill underestimated this kid big time. "I wrote the encryption myself," he said. "You'll never crack it."

They had to come back and ask him for the password.

We now had the makings of the perfect team to emulate real criminal attacks. The big threat to businesses and the public these days is that organised crime has recruited computer whizz kids like Solomon. If I was working with Solomon today on the other side of the law, we would be a lethal combination.

So we formed a second company, called We Fight Fraud.

Solomon and I got on like a house on fire – two peas from the same pod, just from different eras. We could attack businesses in the same way criminals do with Andy overseeing all of our work, and Adam documenting everything and helping to communicate what we did. We were a great team. We could gain some real trust from the big guys and start to make an impact by reducing the crimes that affected so many every day. It's estimated that fraud cost the global economy nearly £4 trillion in 2019, and it's rising all the time. I always wonder how much of it is caused by trauma suffered by most of these guys out there committing crime. I think we should expect a crime wave for years to come after the trauma of 2020 and the Covid-19 pandemic.

For the new-age criminal that robs banks digitally, it's not so much about the money any more, although that's the endgame. Nowadays it's more about the data that leads them to the cash. The thing about data is that everyone has it, from pubs to banks. Just think how many times you gave your information to a bar or restaurant during the Covid-19 lockdown. This, to criminals, is cash. They can target that data held by the company or financial institution, encrypt it and simply just ask the that company for a ransom, to un-encrypt it. The chances of the criminal getting caught are next to nothing, and the gains are in the millions. For digital bank robbers, it's like banks full of cash everywhere.

So to show them how vulnerable they are, we target them just how a criminal gang would, drawing on all of our lived experience. I look at them just as I would if I were hitting them for real with my old team. But this is so much better. I have found my true calling. I have a natural skill, to spot flaws in security systems that others miss. I have been doing it my whole life, looking for the weak spot that can be exploited. On our first job together as the WFF team, we showed the client exactly what our capabilities were.

They commissioned us to do the work for them and on day one, I was sitting outside a branch of a nationwide bank on the high street. My hair was long, my beard scraggly. I hadn't washed for days, and I was begging for change by the cashpoint. I was watching and waiting, looking. The guard was five minutes late for his shift. Those minutes would become massively important, because he had to catch up with time. It meant he was rushing, and not quite on his game. Now I wanted to create more hassle, socially engineer the perfect moment in time that I could exploit. There was a parcel that needed delivering, so after watching the building and learning all the third-party patterns, I knew they never got deliveries before 9 am.

I borrowed my mate's UPS uniform. I had a parcel for every individual bank teller, all of whom I knew worked there because I'd trawled all their social media profiles. At 8:30 I walked through the door, arms packed with parcels. "Come on, bro, you need to help me with these parcels!" I said, walking into the bank's reception.

As the guard came out, Solomon slipped in the door. He was through, into the lift. He shut the door. Went to level two. *That's it, we own the building now.*

The guard came back in and served the rest of his shift. At 6 pm he went home. At 6:05, Solomon disabled the alarm, and we entered as a team.

We planted listening devices on all the phone lines in the bank. Later, I'd be able to hear customer transactions going through. If I wanted, I could generate one-time passcodes from within the bank, the codes for PIN Sentry card readers for online banking. We could generate them at will now, just because of those five minutes. I could access and withdraw the funds from any of that bank's millions of customers.

We left, and there was no trace of us. That's bank robbery in the 21st century. Eight million records, little pieces of data that are the customers of that bank, and the more of it they have, the more value to the criminal. I could grab millions of pieces of data in one hit. Just like the old days, when you think about it: every car I ever got, or bank account, was enabled by information. Nowadays you can buy whole databases for less than a tenner if you know where to look. Today, I would be a different type of criminal. Because real criminals rob other criminals. There's less chance of being arrested. To do that, you have to kidnap somebody and hold them to ransom. Well, ransomware is the same thing. The only difference is, you aren't limited to individuals; you can target huge companies that have the cash to pay. And just like criminals who rob other criminals, it's extremely rare to get caught.

What if I encrypted all of a company's data, locked them out of their email and social media accounts, and didn't let them back in until they paid me? What if I did the same to an individual? How many of you would pay to get back into your Facebook account? Pay me 50 quid and I'll let you back in. You only need a tiny fraction of the 70 million people living in the UK to cough up, and you'd be minted.

Let's think about the information stolen from a company. EasyJet is a recent example. In 2020, they become the victim of a huge data heist, and every person whose data was stolen is now potentially a victim.

Technology companies, especially security companies, get targeted the most – the ones who claim to protect secrets and passwords. Often, the hackers will demand a ransom direct from the companies not to leak all their customers' information. And often, to save their necks, these companies will cough up the ransom money, and keep it all quiet.

We could be encrypting cities.

The victims could be schools or hospitals. If a ransomware gang breaks in and steals all the information about sick or dead children, how much are we as a society willing to pay to make sure that stays private? How many millions? It doesn't matter. Because it's priceless. Personal information is sacrosanct. We should be doing everything within our power to protect it.

That's why we set up We Fight Fraud. We can package our unique talents together and present them to the corporates in a way that shows they're in safe hands. We are able to show companies how to stay safe, and in turn, that keeps all of your information safe.

CHAPTER FORTY-SEVEN

Endgame

Now we've added academics to the We Fight Fraud team, strengthening it even more. I talk to psychologists, criminology lecturers, and experts in the brain and social actions all the time. I always ask them what would have happened if I'd have had structure as a child, if I wasn't passed from pillar to post, if I knew school would give me a career, if when I was asking questions, I wasn't dismissed and treated as a nuisance.

They all answer the same: "You wouldn't be you."

I never wanted to be me. I always wanted to be someone else. That's probably why I was so good at fraud. I felt happy being another person that was not me.

My childhood showed me how not to be as a parent. I would never repeat those mistakes. I was determined to break that cycle. My kids won't follow in my footsteps and end up in a life of crime. Don't get me wrong, they can be mouthy little sods – they are my kids after all! But they're clever, kind, free spirits. They understand that whatever they do on earth, they can be themselves.

Because of this, they are so different from how I was at their age. I can't imagine myself staying in on a Friday night at 18 like they do. And that's all I can ask for.

There are no happy endings in the criminal world. At best, it ends with you looking over your shoulder for the rest of your life. I live with the physical, emotional and psychological scars of it all every day. It still gives me some physical ticks and anxiety, which have all come back while writing this book. They're not positive emotions, and they never really go away. If I could change my past life of excess and criminality for the life of a law-abiding cab driver, knowing what I know now, I would do it in a heartbeat. When you're told your whole life that you're not enough, realising that you are is a revelation.

Perhaps you only ever realise that on the other side, once you've broken the rules, tasted the forbidden fruit. That's why straight people are obsessed with criminals. They say fortune favours the brave. A lot of people are envious of Bonnie and Clyde. And to some extent, perhaps the desire to punish transgression is based on envy. But from my point of view, there is nothing to envy. A life filled with lies and false pretences? The best things in life are real. Only after everything I have been through can I see that. I only ever stole money to cover up my own insecurities. I've learned my lesson: crime does not pay! It's hard work that has got me to where I am now, making the best out of a bad situation.

I've tried to convince others to give it up too, but a man can't tell another man who doesn't have money not to do something to get it. What I can do is point them in the right direction, give them some time, understand what the problems are, and then, hopefully, help them get away from that type of life. Any criminal I have ever known has only ever wanted to be what society deems as normal. Everyone has responsibilities: your primary responsibility is to yourself, and then you can help others too. I've taken a lot of people out of the game, and brought them along on this ride – but only the ones I can totally trust, who won't go back to creating victims. Because you can't be half in, half out. You have to be all out.

I am living proof that if you keep going and believe in yourself, reach for the moon, at least if you fall you will land amongst the stars. What do you have to lose? We all remember an adult telling us when we were younger, "Don't do this" and "Don't do that". Most kids I knew never listened to the advice-giving adults. As a kid you have no worries about the future. We have to figure out a way to give our kids the life skills they need so much. Then we can start to reach our potential as a society.

Every step I have made since 2010 has all been towards one goal. I always knew the power of the media: it is the best form of social engineering that has ever been created. TV has given me a voice, and my story is just one of many kids just like me. And that's what my endgame is all about: helping others. Who knows, one day there may even be a UU: the Underworld University, where kids can get help and advice. If we made a difference to one kid, then it would be worth it!

People often ask me, "Do you think you could go back to crime?" I'm not going to lie, there were times when I had no money and I knew that I could change all that in less than an hour. So yes, of course I thought about it. But instead of committing a crime, I just got another job, and worked harder. All those clichés that you hear are true: you only get out what you put in. If you are lying in a cell reading this, don't ever think it's too late. Only you are in charge of the clock! There is no time like now.

The world I lived in for so long is full of the most amazing people, with the most amazingly creative minds. Most of them just got sucked into that life because of poverty. They were not born bad, although some were born different. They say that money is the root of all evil, but it's actually the route that money makes us take that's the root of evil. People who commit crime have a different path from people who don't. Criminal paths don't just happen; there are always reasons why. The crimes I committed even show why I became a fraudster. I always wanted to be someone else, from the first moment I realised I was not like the others. I just wanted to fit in, but I couldn't. As someone else, I could. Simple.

I have spoken on some of the biggest stages in the world of fraud, globally, with some of the world's most influential people. I have worked on some big TV shows, and have now written my life story. I can honestly say I never thought this would happen to me, but it did. But the proudest moment came for me when, while writing this book, my son Zack went to university.

I broke the circle. Hopefully.